Contents

Introduction 2

Investment Types 21

Government Securities 31

Savings Accounts and CDs – Stability Meets Strategy 43

Gold and Silver – Timeless Investments 53

Investing in Yourself – Turning $100 into Opportunity 62

Real Estate – Building Wealth Brick by Brick 75

Stock Investments - The Cornerstone of Wealth Creation 101

Collectibles – Investing in Nostalgia and Scarcity 143

Cryptocurrency – Digital Gold or Fool's Gold? 161

The Wide World of Other Investments 186

Your Journey Starts Now 192

Glossary of Financial Terms and Acronyms 199

Investment Checklist 206

Sources and Methods 219

Introduction

Why Invest?

Let's face it—most of us aren't rolling in cash. And if you are, congratulations-you've found the wrong book! For the rest of us mere mortals, learning to invest is about making our money work harder than we do. It's not about becoming the next Warren Buffett (although, hey, dream big); it's about building a financial future where you can sleep well at night knowing your dollars are out there hustling, even when you're not.

From Coffee Money to Financial Independence: Meet Sarah

Sarah was a 25-year-old teacher living paycheck to paycheck. She didn't have a high-paying job, but she had something even more valuable: a little curiosity and a determination to take control of her future.

One day, while scrolling through social media, Sarah stumbled upon a post about the power of compounding. The concept was simple: invest a small amount consistently and let time do the heavy lifting. At first, it felt impossible—how could investing just $100 make a difference when her bills seemed endless?

But Sarah made a choice. Instead of buying her weekly fancy coffee, she saved $25 each week. By the end of the month, she had $100. Instead of letting it sit in a low-interest savings account, she took her first step: buying a few shares of an S&P 500 index ETF. It was scary—she had no background in finance and worried about losing her hard-earned money.

Fast forward 10 years: Sarah's small, consistent investments turned into something big... Sarah invested $100 monthly for 10 years. At an 8% average return, her account grew to $18,000—half from compounding. Inspired, she started increasing her contributions as her income grew, and now, Sarah's on track to reach financial independence well before retirement age.

The best part? She never gave up the things she loved—she just found creative ways to save small amounts without sacrificing her lifestyle.

Your Money Deserves a Promotion

Think of your money as your employees. Right now, it's probably just hanging out in a savings account, working a minimum-wage job, earning just enough interest to buy a cup of coffee... in five years. You deserve better than that, and so does your money. Investing gives your dollars a chance to upgrade their career—to go from barista to CEO, growing and compounding over time.

For example, if you start with just $100 and invest it wisely, it could double, triple, or even quadruple in value over a few decades. Sure, it's not going to pay off your mortgage tomorrow, but it's a start. And great things start small—just ask any oak tree.

Financial Independence: The Ultimate Glow-Up

Let's dream for a second. Imagine a life where you're not tied to your 9-to-5, checking your bank account nervously the day before payday. Investing is the bridge to that life. With every dollar you invest, you're planting a seed that can grow into financial independence. Over time, your investments can generate income on their own, giving you the freedom to live life on your terms.

Want to travel? Start your own business? Spend more time with family? That's the beauty of financial independence—you call the shots. And all it takes to start is $100, a bit of knowledge, and the willingness to try.

Opportunities are Everywhere

Investing doesn't have to be complicated. It's not about memorizing stock tickers or predicting the next big market crash like some Wall Street wizard. It's about putting your money into things that grow—stocks, bonds, real estate, and yes, even that thing called cryptocurrency (but we'll get to that).

The beauty of today's world is that anyone can invest. You don't need a fancy suit, a six-figure salary, or insider knowledge. All you need is access to the internet, a few bucks, and maybe some coffee to fuel your research.

Procrastination: The Costliest Mistake

"I'll start investing when I have more money." Sound familiar? The truth is, the longer you wait, the harder it gets.

Time is the secret sauce of investing, and starting early is like adding extra seasoning—it makes everything better.

For example, if you start investing $100 a month at age 25, you could have over $250,000 by retirement (assuming a 7% annual return). Wait until you're 35, and you'd end up with less than half of that. The math doesn't lie—your future self will either thank you or send you a strongly worded letter of disappointment.

The Power of Compounding

Compounding is like the eighth wonder of the world—simple yet astonishing. It's the process where your money earns returns, and then those returns start earning returns of their own. Think of it as a snowball rolling down a hill: it starts small, but as it picks up more snow, it grows bigger and faster with every turn. For example, if you invest $100 today and earn 10% annually, in 20 years you'll have $672.75. That is over 6 times the initial investment! It gets better, if you start with $100 and add $100 per month at that same rate of return, you will have $72,498.67. Not too bad for just the price you probably pay for streaming services.

With compounding, those returns build on themselves, your investment can grow exponentially. The best part? The earlier you start; the more time compounding has to work its magic. It's not about timing the market; it's about giving time to your money in the market.

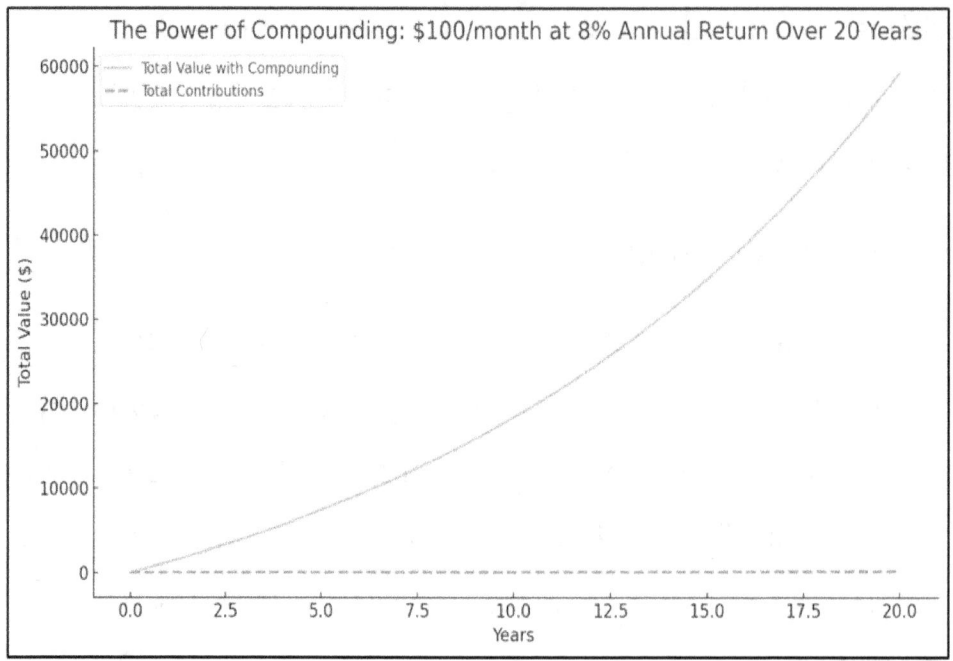

Figure 1: The power of compounding with $100 monthly investment.

Inflation: The Silent Thief

You know that annoying friend who always "borrows" money and conveniently forgets to pay it back? But unlike your friend, inflation doesn't just forget; it shows up at your doorstep every year, demanding more from you while leaving less in return. It's the roommate no one asked for!

That's inflation - it steals your future buying power. What costs you $1 today could cost $2 in a few years. Left unchecked, inflation quietly erodes the value of your hard-earned cash while you're busy binge-watching your favorite shows.

Investing is your way to fight back. By putting your money into assets that grow faster than inflation—like stocks, real estate, or even gold—you're not just protecting your money; you're giving it the tools to outrun inflation and maybe even lap it a few times.

In the chart below, you can see that even with the lowest inflation rate of 2.5%, your $100 loses nearly 40% of its value over 20 years. Meaning that if you want to buy that car that costs $50,000 today, you can expect to pay nearly $82,000 after 20 years. If inflation spikes and averages 5%, that same $100 loses over 62% of its value – which means that car will cost over $132,000. Ouch!

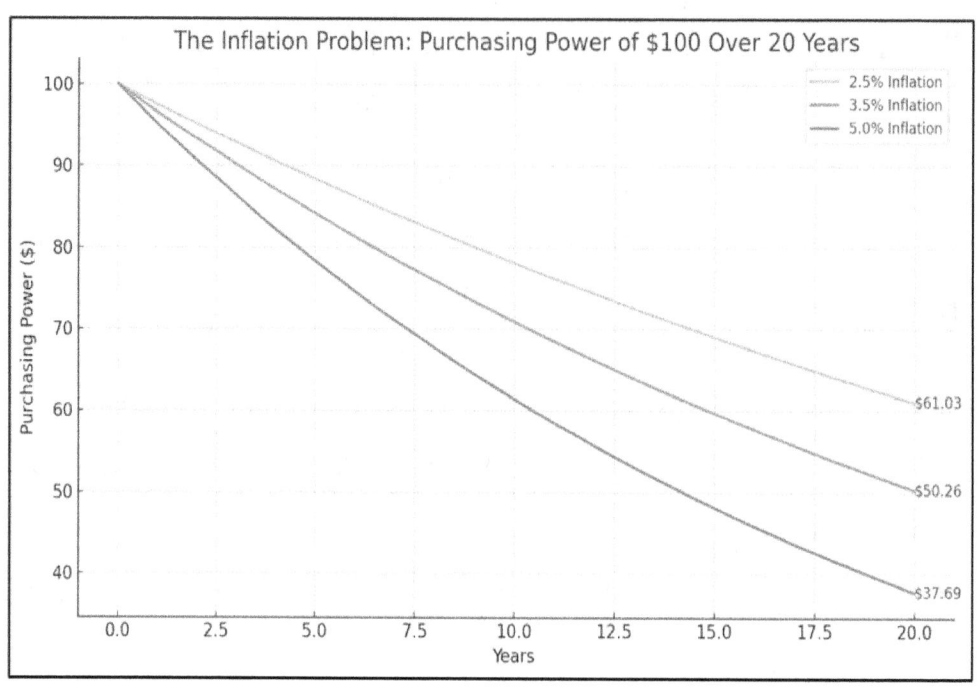

Figure 2: Shows the decay in purchasing power of $100 over time.

The Best Time to Start is Yesterday. The Second Best Time is Now.

Investing isn't about perfection—it's about progress. You don't need to know everything to begin; you just need to take the first step. This book is here to guide you, demystify the jargon, and maybe even make you laugh a little along the way. Whether you're starting with $100 or $1,000, the principles are the same: Start small, be consistent, and let time and compounding work their magic.

So, grab a cup of coffee, settle in, and let's start building a financial future you can be proud of. And remember, every expert investor was once a beginner too—you're in good company.

Understanding Risk and Reward

Investing is a bit like dating. Every opportunity comes with a mix of excitement and uncertainty, and the key to success lies in finding the right balance for *you*. Too much risk? You could end up heartbroken—or worse, broke. Too little risk? Your money might never grow, leaving you stuck in financial limbo. The trick is to understand the stakes and play your cards wisely, all while keeping the rest of your financial life in check.

What is Risk? And Why Does It Matter?

Risk is the possibility that things won't go as planned. It's the rollercoaster ride of investing—the stomach drops, the unexpected turns, the occasional upside-down moment. But just like a rollercoaster, risk is what makes the journey exciting and, ultimately, rewarding. The higher the risk, the greater the potential reward—but also the greater the chance of losses.

For example, investing in government savings bonds is like riding the carousel: calm, predictable, and unlikely to leave you dizzy. On the other hand, dabbling in cryptocurrency? That's the financial equivalent of strapping into the world's fastest coaster with your eyes closed.

Understanding what level of risk you can handle is a critical first step—and spoiler alert: it's different for everyone.

What About Reward?

Reward is what we're all here for, right? It's the light at the end of the financial tunnel. But here's the deal: not every investment pays off equally. Low-risk investments, like savings accounts or government bonds, typically offer modest but steady returns. Higher-risk options, like stocks or real estate, come with the chance for higher returns—but also the possibility of short-term losses.

The good news? By carefully balancing risk and reward, you can build a portfolio that suits your goals and your nerves. And no, it doesn't have to involve pulling all-nighters watching stock market charts.

It's About Balance, Not All or Nothing

Before you dive into the deep end of investing, take a step back and look at the big picture—your *entire* financial life. Investing is just one piece of the puzzle, and it only works if the rest of your financial house is in order. Here are a few things to consider before risking a single dollar:

Emergency Fund = Safety Net

Life happens, and it's usually expensive. Whether it's a surprise car repair or an unexpected medical bill, having 3–6 months' worth of living expenses in an easily accessible account can save you from financial stress. Think of it as your financial parachute—because you never know when you might need to pull the cord.

Cash Flow is King

1. Investing is important, but so is paying your bills. Make sure your monthly income covers your necessary expenses *and* leaves room for savings before allocating money to investments. Otherwise, you might find yourself selling stocks at the worst possible time—like during a market downturn—to cover rent.

Debt: Friend or Frenemy?

Not all debt is created equal. High-interest debt, like credit cards, should be tackled before you start investing. Why? Because no investment can guarantee a return higher than the 20% interest your credit card company is charging. (And if it does, it's probably illegal.)

Know Thyself: Your Personal Risk Tolerance

Everyone has a different appetite for risk. Some people thrive on the thrill of high-stakes investments, while others would rather play it safe and avoid sleepless nights. Your risk tolerance depends on several factors, including:

- **Your Time Horizon**: The longer you can leave your money invested, the more risk you can take on. If you need the cash in a year, stick to lower-risk options. If you're investing for retirement 30 years down the road, you've got time to ride out the bumps.
- **Your Financial Goals**: Are you saving for a dream vacation in five years or building a retirement fund? Your goals will influence how much risk you should take.
- **Your Personality**: Let's be real—some people just aren't built for high-risk strategies. If market swings give you heart palpitations, that's a sign to dial it back.

The Balanced Approach

Investing isn't about going all-in on one wild idea (unless you really want to test your luck). It's about creating a diversified plan that fits your overall financial picture. Think of it as building a financial buffet: a little bit of safety, a dash of growth, and just enough spice to keep things interesting. Here's how to approach it:

- **Start with Stability**: Low-risk investments, like savings accounts or bonds, create a solid foundation.
- **Add Growth Opportunities**: Stocks and real estate offer long-term potential for higher returns.
- **Sprinkle in Some High-Risk Bets**: Cryptocurrencies or collectibles can add excitement—but only with money you can afford to lose.

Are You Financially Fit to Start Investing? Let's Check.

Before diving into the world of investing, it's important to understand where you stand financially and what your goals are. This quick questionnaire helps you assess your readiness to start investing and pinpoint areas that may need improvement.

Financial Readiness Questionnaire:

Answer the following questions to evaluate your financial readiness and goals:

1. **Emergency Savings:** Do you have at least 3-6 months' worth of living expenses saved?
   - ☐ Yes
   - ☐ No

2. **Debt Status:** Do you have high-interest debt (e.g., credit card balances) that you're working to pay off?
   - ☐ Yes
   - ☐ No

3. **Investment Horizon:** When do you plan to use the money you'll invest?
   - ☐ Short-term (1-3 years)
   - ☐ Medium-term (4-10 years)
   - ☐ Long-term (10+ years)

4. **Risk Comfort:** How comfortable are you with temporary declines in your investments?
   - ☐ Very comfortable (I can ride out big market swings)

- ☐ Somewhat comfortable (Minor dips make me uneasy)
- ☐ Not comfortable (I don't want to see losses)

1. **Monthly Budget:** Can you consistently set aside $25–$100 (or more) each month to invest?

- ☐ Yes
- ☐ No

1. **Knowledge and Learning:** Are you willing to spend some time learning about investing basics?

- ☐ Yes
- ☐ No

If you answered **"No"** to any questions—don't worry! Investing doesn't require perfection. Use this as a guide to build a strong foundation, such as prioritizing high-interest debt repayment or creating an emergency fund. Remember, starting small and starting now is the key to long-term success. Even if you're learning as you go, every step forward is progress.

No Emergency Fund? Start Small

If you're eager to invest but don't have a full safety net yet, you might consider allocating part of your savings into fully liquid, low-risk investments that can be sold quickly if needed. Options include:

- **High-Yield Savings Accounts**: Safe and accessible while earning a small return.
- **Money Market Funds**: Low-risk with slightly higher yields.
- **Short-Term Government Bonds or T-Bills**: Provide stability and can be sold easily.

This approach lets you dip your toes into investing while keeping your funds accessible in case life throws you a curveball.

Definitely Payoff Your High-Yield Credit Cards

Before you invest, check if you're carrying high-interest credit card debt. Why? Because paying off a credit card with a 20% interest rate is like getting a guaranteed 20% return on your money—something no safe investment can promise.

Here's an example:

- Imagine you owe $1,000 on a credit card with a 20% annual interest rate.
- By paying it off, you save $200 in interest charges each year. That's like earning a 20% return on a $1,000 investment, risk-free!

While investing is exciting, paying down high-interest debt is often the smartest first step. Once that debt is gone, you'll have more money to invest and a clearer path to financial growth.

Financial Foundation and Starting Your Journey

Every great journey starts with a solid foundation, and investing is no different. Before you take your first step, it's essential to have a clear financial base—a safety net that allows you to move forward with confidence. Think of it like building a house: without a strong foundation, even the most impressive structures can crumble. Whether it's a well-stocked emergency fund or freedom from high-interest debt, this groundwork isn't about perfection but about giving yourself the stability to take on new opportunities without fear.

Because here's the truth: **risk is inevitable**. There is no reward without risk. The stock market will have its ups and downs, and no investment—no matter how safe—comes without some uncertainty. But that's what makes the journey worth it. By understanding the balance between risk and reward, you'll learn to navigate these challenges, turning fear of the unknown into opportunities for growth. Every step you take, no matter how small, is progress toward your goal of financial freedom. Remember, this is your journey—one that's not defined by how quickly you get there, but by the courage you show to start and the commitment to keep moving forward.

Investment Types

Investing is a journey with many paths, each offering its own set of rewards and challenges. Some investments are as steady as a rock, while others are thrilling rides that can leave you exhilarated—or dizzy. This chapter introduces the most common types of investments, from the ultra-safe to the high-stakes, helping you understand their requirements, returns, and risks. While every type has its place, this book emphasizes options that allow you to start with as little as $100, making investing accessible no matter where you're starting.

Capital Requirements

"How much do I need to get started?" This is one of the first questions many new investors ask. The answer depends on the type of investment. While some categories like real estate or collectibles require substantial upfront capital, others, like stocks or savings bonds, offer opportunities to start with as little as $100. This section explores the capital requirements for various investment types, covering both the high-priced and more accessible options, so you can see where your financial resources fit in.

High-Priced Investments: Real Estate and Collectibles

Certain investment types, like real estate and collectibles, come with high entry costs. Buying a rental property often requires a significant down payment, closing costs, and reserves for maintenance and repairs. Depending on the market, you might need tens of thousands of dollars to even get started. Similarly, high-value collectibles—such as rare coins, vintage trading cards, or fine art—can cost anywhere from thousands to millions of dollars, making them less accessible to most beginners.

That said, fractional ownership has opened the door to these markets. Today, platforms allow you to invest in shares of real estate or collectibles with far less capital—sometimes as little as $10 or $20. While this book focuses on investments accessible with $100, it's good to know these high-ticket options are becoming more approachable.

Savings Bonds, Treasury Bonds, and Bank Accounts

For low-risk investments, U.S. savings bonds and Treasury bonds are great options. The minimum purchase amount for a Treasury bond is $100 when buying through the TreasuryDirect website. U.S. savings bonds, like Series I or Series EE bonds, also have a $25 minimum, making them accessible for smaller investors. These options offer predictable, stable returns and are a safe way to preserve capital.

Bank accounts and Certificates of Deposit (CDs) have minimal capital requirements, with most banks allowing you to open a savings account with $25 to $100. CDs typically require a minimum deposit of $500 to $1,000, but there are some banks and credit unions offering CDs for as little as $100. While these options offer low risk, their returns are modest, often barely outpacing inflation. Still, they are a good starting point for building an emergency fund or parking cash safely

Stock Market Basics: Breaking Barriers with $100

The stock market is one of the most accessible ways to grow your wealth, even if you're starting small. Thanks to fractional shares, you can buy a portion of high-priced stocks like Amazon or Google for as little as $100. Beginner-friendly options like ETFs (Exchange-Traded Funds) also offer affordable entry points. Many ETFs trade for under $100 and provide instant diversification across sectors.

Modern brokerages—including Robinhood, Fidelity, and Charles Schwab—have removed minimum balance requirements, making it easy for new investors to get started. With just a smartphone and an internet connection, the stock market is within reach.

However, there are rules and limitations you should know. The Pattern Day Trading (PDT) Rule, for instance, requires a minimum balance of $25,000 to engage in frequent day trading. This rule applies if you make more than four day trades within a rolling five-day period. While this may seem restrictive, it's designed to protect investors from excessive risk. Fortunately, long-term investing strategies like buying and holding stocks or ETFs don't require such high balances and are more suitable for beginners.

Accessible Investing for All

The beauty of today's investing world is that technology has torn down many of the barriers that once kept beginners out. You no longer need thousands of dollars or an advanced degree in finance to start investing. All you need is a small amount of money, like $100, and the willingness to learn. This book will focus on investment options that align with these realities, guiding you to make the most of what you have while keeping an eye on what's possible for the future.

The bottom line? Whether you're working with $100 or dreaming of larger investments, the most important step is starting. Every investor begins somewhere, and $100 is more than enough to take that first step toward financial independence.

Rates of Return

When it comes to investing, everyone wants to know, "What's in it for me?" Rates of return are the payoff, but they come in two flavors: current income and appreciation. Current income is like the paycheck you receive for showing up—steady, reliable, and consistent. Appreciation, on the other hand, is the promotion you work hard for, the long-term reward that builds over time as your investment grows in value. Together, these two components determine the overall return on your investment.

Current Income

Some investments are built to pay you back immediately, in regular, predictable amounts. Think of government bonds, savings accounts, or dividend-paying stocks. These generate current income—interest payments, rental income, or dividends—that provide cash flow while you still hold the investment. For example, a corporate bond might pay 4% annually, giving you $40 in income for every $1,000 invested, while a blue-chip stock might deliver dividends that you can either pocket or reinvest. These investments can feel like the warm blanket of your portfolio, offering comfort and stability.

Current income can be particularly important for those looking to supplement their regular earnings or fund short-term needs without selling their investments. However, income-focused investments typically have lower rates of appreciation, meaning they grow more slowly over time. It's all about balance—earning today while keeping an eye on the future.

Appreciation

Appreciation is where things get exciting. This is the increase in the value of your investment over time, and it's the driving force behind long-term wealth creation. Stocks are the poster child for appreciation, as companies grow and increase in value. Real estate also shines here, with properties often appreciating due to market trends, improvements, or inflation.

For example, if you buy $100 worth of stock today and its value grows by 10% each year, it will be worth over $670 in 20 years. That's the magic of appreciation: it compounds on itself, creating exponential growth. However, appreciation-focused investments often require patience—they're the marathon runners of your portfolio, not the sprinters.

It's important to note that appreciation isn't guaranteed. Stocks can drop, real estate markets can crash, and speculative investments like cryptocurrency can see wild swings. That's why diversification—spreading your money across different types of investments—is key to managing these risks.

Balancing Current Income and Appreciation

Most investors don't live in an all-or-nothing world. Instead, the ideal portfolio balances investments that provide current income with those that offer appreciation potential. For example, you might combine dividend-paying stocks (income) with growth stocks (appreciation) to capture the best of both worlds. Or pair rental properties (income) with real estate investments that you plan to flip or hold long-term for value growth.

Your personal financial goals, time horizon, and risk tolerance will determine the right mix. If you're young and building wealth, you might focus more on appreciation, letting time and compounding do the heavy lifting. If you're nearing retirement, income-producing investments may take center stage, ensuring you have a steady stream of cash while preserving your principal.

Risk Factors

If rates of return are the reward, risk is the price of admission. Each investment type carries unique risks. Government bonds, for example, are almost risk-free, but their returns can barely keep up with inflation. Stocks and real estate, on the other hand, come with market volatility, while cryptocurrency can swing from riches to rags in a single day. Understanding these risks is crucial to making informed decisions. We'll break down the risk factors for each type of investment and discuss strategies to manage them. The goal isn't to avoid risk altogether—it's to embrace the right risks for your financial goals.

The Risk Scale: 0 to 5

To make it easier to evaluate investments, this book uses a **Risk Scale** ranging from **0 to 5**:

- **0 - No Risk**: Investments with guaranteed capital protection, such as government bonds.
- **1 - Minimal Risk**: Low-risk options like CDs or high-yield savings accounts.
- **2 - Low Risk**: Conservative choices such as corporate bonds or precious metals.
- **3 - Moderate Risk**: Stocks and real estate with higher growth potential but increased volatility.
- **4 - High Risk**: Investments like collectibles or individual growth stocks with significant upside but more unpredictability.
- **5 - Very High Risk**: Speculative markets like cryptocurrency with extreme potential for both gains and losses.

This scale isn't just a tool—it's your guide to making smarter investment decisions. By understanding where each investment falls, you can create a balanced portfolio that reflects your financial goals and risk tolerance. Think of it like planning a meal: you wouldn't make every dish spicy—you'd balance it with something mild and satisfying.

This chapter sets the foundation for exploring the world of investments. Whether you're looking to start with $100 or considering larger contributions in the future, knowing the different types and how they fit into your plan is the first step to building wealth. With that in mind, let's dive into the details of each type and discover how you can start investing today.

Government Securities – Help Out Uncle Sam

Warning: This chapter should not be read while operating heavy machinery! Ok, they are not flashy but Government securities are the backbone of low-risk investing, offering unparalleled safety and dependability. When your politicians are spending money that out government doesn't have, this is one of the ways they do it. They borrow it from us. These investments are backed by the U.S. government, which has never defaulted on its debt, making them one of the most secure options available to investors. Of course, default is extremely unlikely, especially when you can just print cash to payoff these securities. Not exactly how it works but now you know why these are near zero risk. So, whether you're just starting out or looking for a stable way to preserve your wealth, government securities provide a straightforward path to predictable returns with minimal risk.

Government securities come in several forms, including Treasury bonds, Treasury notes, Treasury bills, and U.S. savings bonds. Each type serves a unique purpose, from long-term income generation to short-term liquidity. Together, they form the foundation for conservative investing, giving you peace of mind while your money works steadily in the background.

Types of Government Securities

Government securities are diverse enough to meet a variety of financial needs. Treasury bonds, often referred to as T-bonds, are long-term investments with maturities ranging from 20 to 30 years. These bonds pay interest semi-annually, making them a popular choice for investors seeking a steady income stream over decades. While T-bonds require a long-term commitment, they also offer higher interest rates compared to shorter-term securities, making them attractive for those with a longer investment horizon.

Treasury notes, or T-notes, are medium-term securities with maturities between 2 and 10 years. Like T-bonds, they pay interest every six months, but they offer greater liquidity due to their shorter timeframes. T-notes strike a balance between income generation and flexibility, making them ideal for investors who want predictable returns without tying up their funds for decades.

Treasury bills, or T-bills, are the shortest-term option, with maturities ranging from a few days to one year. Unlike bonds and notes, T-bills don't pay regular interest. Instead, they are sold at a discount to their face value and pay the full amount upon maturity. For example, you might purchase a T-bill for $950 and receive $1,000 when it matures. This structure makes T-bills a favorite for those who need a safe place to park cash while earning modest returns.

U.S. savings bonds, including Series I and Series EE bonds, are another excellent option for low-risk investors. Series I bonds are designed to protect against inflation, offering a combination of a fixed rate and an inflation-adjusted rate. These bonds are particularly valuable during periods of rising prices, ensuring your investment maintains its purchasing power. Series EE bonds, on the other hand, are guaranteed to double in value if held for 20 years, providing a predictable return for long-term savers.

How Mark Protected His Savings with Series I Bonds

Mark, a 45-year-old small business owner, had always been careful with his money. After years of hard work, he had built up a modest cash reserve of $10,000. In early 2022, Mark started to notice prices rising everywhere—at the gas pump, the grocery store, and even for materials in his business. Inflation was eating away at his purchasing power, and he realized that leaving his money in a traditional savings account earning less than 1% interest meant he was effectively losing money.

After a bit of research, Mark discovered Series I bonds, a government-backed investment designed to protect against inflation. Series I bonds pay a fixed interest rate plus an inflation-adjusted rate that changes twice a year. In 2022, with inflation hitting 7-9%, the bonds offered a record-breaking annualized yield of over **9%**—far outpacing traditional savings accounts.

Mark decided to invest $10,000 into Series I bonds through TreasuryDirect.gov. Over the next year, his investment grew steadily, earning interest that kept up with rising costs. While he knew the rate would eventually adjust as inflation cooled, the bonds gave him peace of mind. Not only was his money protected, but it was also growing—something that felt like a win in uncertain economic times.

For Mark, Series I bonds weren't a get-rich-quick solution, but they were the perfect tool to preserve his purchasing power and shield his savings from the silent thief of inflation.

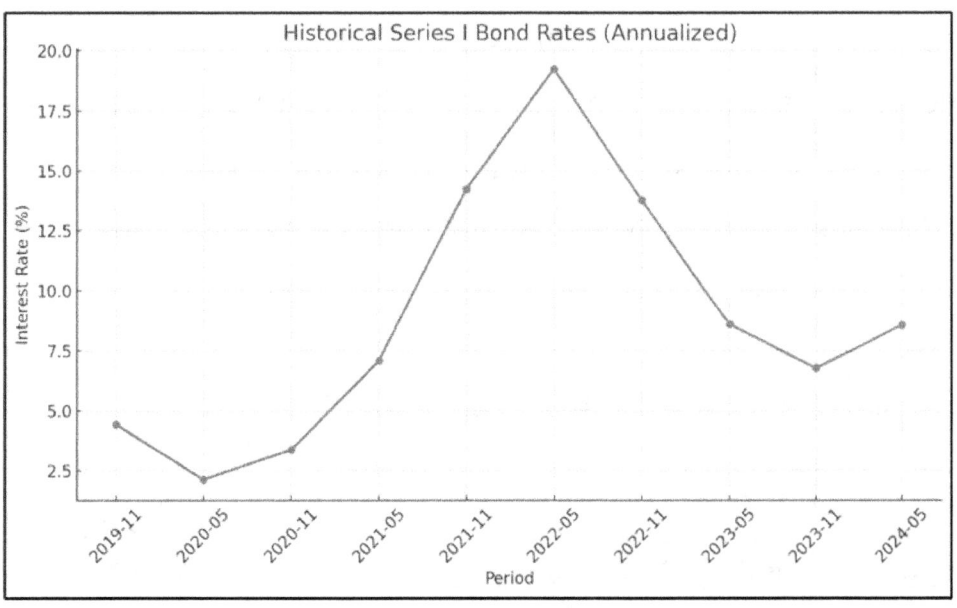

Figure 3: Historical Rates of Inflation Adjusted Series I U.S. Bonds

Capital Requirements

One of the most appealing aspects of government securities is their accessibility. You can begin investing in Treasury bonds, notes, or bills with as little as $100, making them an excellent choice for beginners. U.S. savings bonds are even more approachable, with a minimum investment of just $25 for electronic purchases. This low barrier to entry allows you to start small while building a foundation for your financial future.

For those who can invest larger amounts, government securities remain an attractive option. Whether you're looking to deploy substantial capital or simply start with $100, these investments provide stability and flexibility that fit into any financial plan.

Type of Security	Term	Minimum	Maximum
Treasury Bonds	20 - 30 years	$100	No Limit
Treasury Notes	2 - 10 years	$100	No Limit
Treasury Bills	A few days to 1 year	$100	No Limit
Series I Savings Bond	Up to 30 years	$25	$10,000/year
Series EE Savings Bor	Up to 30 years	$25	$10,000/year

Figure 4: Chart of Government Securities

Rates of Return

The returns on government securities vary depending on the type and maturity. T-bills, being short-term instruments, generally offer lower returns, often slightly higher than savings account rates. T-notes and T-bonds, with their longer maturities, provide higher yields in exchange for tying up your money for a longer period. For example, current rates on T-bonds may range from 3% to 4%, depending on the term and market conditions.

The differing rates among bond terms, is known as the Yield Curve and can be represented graphically with interest rates on bonds with different maturities, typically U.S. Treasury bonds. It shows how much return investors can expect for lending money over short, medium, and long periods. A normal yield curve slopes upward, reflecting that longer-term bonds pay higher interest rates than short-term bonds. This is because investors demand more compensation for tying up their money for extended periods and taking on greater risks, like inflation or economic uncertainty. For example, a 2-year Treasury might yield 2%, while a 10-year Treasury could yield 3.5%. A normal yield curve is often seen during periods of economic growth, as it signals investor confidence in the future and the expectation of rising interest rates over time. When this curve flattens or inverts, however, it can be a sign of economic stress or an impending slowdown.

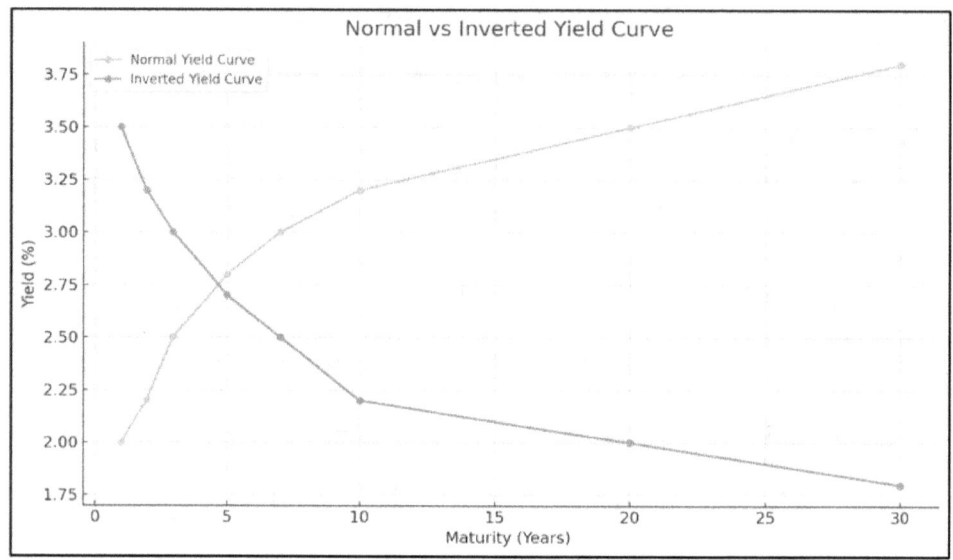

Figure 5: U.S. Government Yield Curves (Typical vs Inverted)

U.S. Savings Bond Rates

U.S. savings bonds also deliver dependable returns. Series I bonds adjust their rates twice a year to keep pace with inflation, making them particularly valuable during periods of rising prices. Series EE bonds, while fixed in their returns, offer the security of knowing your investment will double if held to maturity.

While government securities don't offer the high returns of stocks or real estate, they excel in preserving capital and generating steady income. They are less about dramatic growth and more about providing the financial stability every portfolio needs.

Keep in mind that Savings Bonds, both Series I and Series EE have an early redemption penalty where the bonds will forfeit their last 3 months of interest if redeemed before 5 years.

Risk Factors

Despite their reputation for safety, government securities are not entirely risk-free. Fixed-rate securities, like Treasury bonds and notes, are susceptible to inflation risk. If inflation rises significantly, the purchasing power of the interest payments and principal may decrease. This is why Series I bonds, which adjust for inflation, can be an essential tool in combating this risk.

Another consideration is interest rate risk. Bond prices move inversely to interest rates, meaning that if rates rise, the value of your existing bonds may fall. However, this is only a concern if you need to sell the bond before it matures. For those holding bonds to maturity, the government guarantees both the interest payments and the return of the principal.

Finally, liquidity risk is a minor concern for savings bonds. While they can be redeemed early, doing so within the first five years will result in a penalty equivalent to three months' interest. This makes them slightly less flexible than other government securities but still a reliable option for long-term savers.

How to Invest in Government Securities

Investing in government securities is simpler than ever. The U.S. Treasury's online platform, TreasuryDirect, allows you to purchase Treasury bonds, notes, bills, and savings bonds directly with no fees. TreasuryDirect is user-friendly and accessible, making it the go-to option for many investors.

Alternatively, you can purchase government securities through brokerage accounts, which often provide access to secondary markets where you can buy and sell these investments. While brokerages may charge fees, they offer added flexibility and the ability to trade securities before maturity.

The Role of Government Securities in Your Portfolio

Investing in government securities is like taking a nap: not much happens, but you wake up feeling slightly better about your financial life. Just don't expect any dreams of wild gains. Government securities can be an essential component of any balanced portfolio. They provide a counterbalance to riskier investments, offering stability and reliable income. For beginners, they are an excellent way to build confidence and grow wealth steadily, all while preserving your capital.

Whether you're using T-bills as a safe place to park cash, T-bonds for long-term income, or Series I bonds to combat inflation, government securities offer versatility and dependability. They might not deliver the excitement of stocks or crypto, but their predictability is their strength.

Government securities are proof that boring can be beautiful. They're steady, reliable, and a cornerstone of smart investing. Whether you're just starting with $100 or adding stability to a diversified portfolio, these investments ensure your financial journey begins with a solid foundation.

Here is the website for TreasuryDirect:

https://www.treasurydirect.gov

Savings Accounts and CDs – Stability Meets Strategy

Savings accounts and Certificates of Deposit (CDs) are the financial equivalent of comfort food—familiar, dependable, and perfect for those seeking security. While they may not offer the dazzling returns of stocks or the thrill of cryptocurrency, they are critical tools for preserving capital and growing your money in a low-risk environment. Whether you're building an emergency fund, saving for a short-term goal, or looking for a steady, reliable return, these options have you covered.

Savings Accounts: A Flexible Foundation

Savings accounts are where many people begin their financial journeys, offering liquidity, safety, and modest interest rates. They're perfect for short-term goals or storing cash for emergencies. While nearly every bank offers savings accounts, the rates and terms can vary dramatically depending on the institution.

- **Traditional Banks (Money Center Banks)**: Large institutions like Chase, Bank of America, and Wells Fargo provide convenience with a vast network of branches and ATMs. However, their interest rates tend to hover at the lower end of the spectrum, often below **0.5%**, making them more suited for convenience than competitive returns.
- **Community Banks and Credit Unions**: These smaller, locally focused institutions often provide better rates than their larger counterparts, especially for loyal customers. Credit unions, in particular, can be a great option because they are member-owned and often offer savings account rates closer to **1%**.
- **Online Banks**: The standout in the savings account world is the growing class of online-only banks.

Institutions like SoFi, Ally Bank, and Marcus by Goldman Sachs consistently offer high-yield savings accounts with interest rates of **4% or higher**, often with no fees and low minimum balances. These banks achieve higher yields by cutting out the costs associated with maintaining physical branches.

Emergency Funds: Why They Belong in Savings Accounts

Before diving into CDs or other investments, every investor should prioritize an emergency fund. A good rule of thumb is to save three to six months' worth of living expenses. Because emergencies don't wait, this money should remain easily accessible, and savings accounts are ideal for this purpose. They provide a safe, liquid option that allows you to withdraw funds instantly without penalties.

Certificates of Deposit (CDs): Higher Returns for Commitment

For those willing to lock away their money for a set period, CDs offer a chance to earn higher interest rates than savings accounts. When you invest in a CD, you agree to leave your money untouched for a specific term, which can range from a few months to several years. In return, the bank rewards you with a higher, fixed interest rate.

Rates for CDs vary based on the term and the financial institution:

- **Traditional Banks**: These offer standard CD rates, but their returns are generally lower compared to other options. For example, a 1-year CD at a money center bank might yield 2%, compared to 4% or more at an online bank.
- **Online Banks**: Once again, online institutions like SoFi, Discover, and CIT Bank take the lead, offering competitive CD rates. Their streamlined operations and lack of physical branches allow them to pass the savings onto you. Current rates for a 1-year CD can exceed **4%**.
- **Brokered Deposits**: Available through brokerage accounts, brokered CDs are another compelling option. These are special CDs issued by banks to attract deposits from brokerage customers. They often feature rates that are higher than those offered directly by the bank. For instance, brokerages like Fidelity, Schwab, and Vanguard regularly list CDs with

terms ranging from 3 months to 5 years, offering rates that can be significantly more attractive than traditional or online banks.

Minimum Requirements: Savings for All Budgets

The accessibility of savings accounts and CDs makes them great starting points for all types of investors. Most savings accounts require a minimum deposit of just $25 to $100, and some online banks have no minimums at all. CDs traditionally require a higher initial deposit, often starting at $500 to $1,000, but many online banks now offer CDs with minimums as low as $100, putting them within reach for most people.

Rates of Return: What You Can Expect

While savings accounts are highly liquid, their returns are modest. Rates at traditional banks often hover below **0.5%**, while credit unions and online banks push that figure closer to **4%** or higher for high-yield savings accounts. CDs offer a step up, with current rates for a 1-year term ranging from 2% at traditional banks to over 4% at online banks or through brokered deposits.

Longer-term CDs—such as 3-year or 5-year options—tend to offer even higher rates, but they require a greater commitment. If you're considering locking up your funds for the long term, make sure you won't need the money during the term, as early withdrawals often result in penalties.

Where to Open Accounts and Buy CDs

Opening a savings account or CD is straightforward, and the options are plentiful.

- **Traditional Banks**: If you value convenience and in-person support, traditional banks like Chase or Wells Fargo are solid choices, though their rates may not be the most competitive.
- **Community Banks and Credit Unions**: These institutions often provide more personalized service and better rates, especially for members or local customers.
- **Online Banks**: SoFi, Ally, Marcus, and Discover lead the charge in high-yield options. Their competitive rates, low fees, and easy account setup make them perfect for digital-savvy investors.
- **Brokered Deposits**: If you already have a brokerage account, brokered CDs from Fidelity, Schwab, or

Vanguard offer a way to earn competitive rates while keeping all your investments in one place.

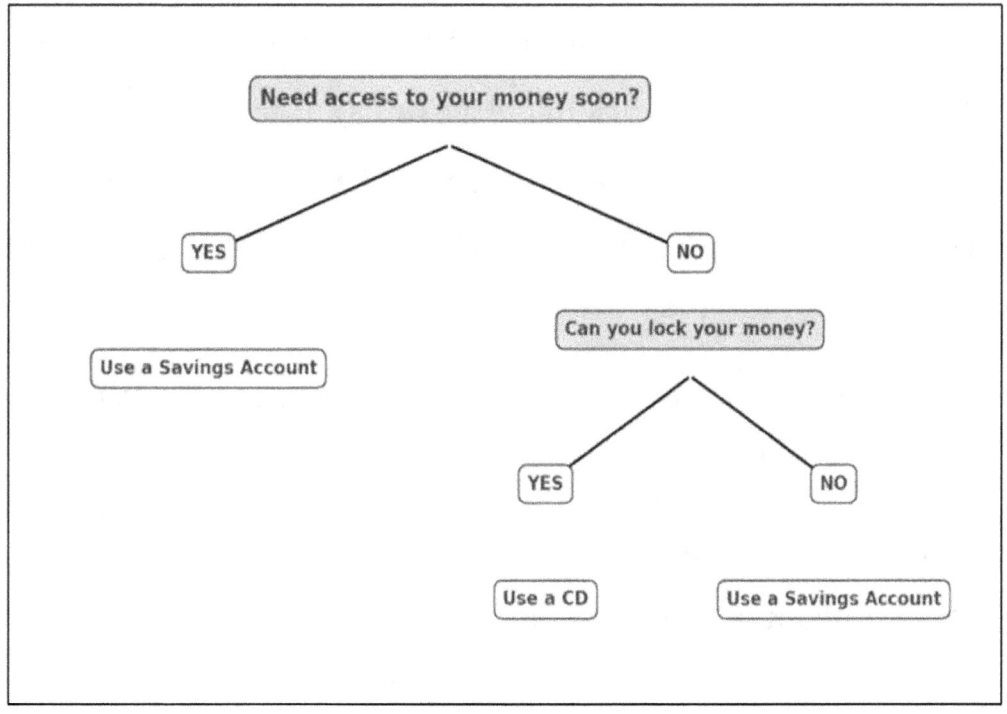

Figure 6: Savings versus CD Decision Chart

CD Ladders: A Strategy for Flexibility and Growth

Certificates of Deposit (CDs) offer safety and predictable returns, but one downside is that your money is locked up for a set period. That's where a CD ladder comes in—a smart strategy to balance earning higher interest rates with maintaining regular access to your money.

A CD ladder works by dividing your money into multiple CDs with staggered maturity dates. For example, instead of putting $10,000 into a single 5-year CD, you could split it across 1-year, 2-year, 3-year, 4-year, and 5-year CDs. As each CD matures, you can choose to reinvest the money into a new 5-year CD (to lock in better rates) or use it for expenses. This way, you'll always have access to a portion of your money annually while still taking advantage of longer-term, higher interest rates.

John's Smart Strategy: Using a CD Ladder for Steady Income and Flexibility

Meet John, a 65-year-old retiree who wants a safe and steady income to supplement his Social Security. John has $50,000 in savings, and instead of locking it all up in a single CD, he decides to build a 5-year CD ladder:

- He splits his $50,000 evenly into five CDs:
- $10,000 into a 1-year CD at 2.5% interest.
- $10,000 into a 2-year CD at 3.0% interest.
- $10,000 into a 3-year CD at 3.2% interest.
- $10,000 into a 4-year CD at 3.4% interest.
- $10,000 into a 5-year CD at 3.7% interest.

After the first year, the 1-year CD matures. Instead of spending the money, John reinvests it into a new 5-year CD at the current rate. The next year, the 2-year CD matures, and he repeats the process. Over time, John now has a CD maturing every year, giving him:

1. Regular access to cash to handle unexpected expenses.
2. The opportunity to reinvest at higher rates if interest rates rise.
3. Higher overall returns compared to putting all his money in short-term CDs.

CD ladders are ideal for retirees like John or anyone who values a balance between safety, growth, and flexibility. By using this strategy, you'll avoid locking all your money up while still earning more than a savings account offers.

Risk Scale: 0 to 1

On the Risk Scale, savings accounts and CDs are as close to risk-free as you can get. Your deposits are protected up to $250,000 per account through FDIC insurance for banks and NCUA insurance for credit unions. The primary risk with these investments is inflation: while your principal is safe, the returns may not keep pace with rising prices, eroding your purchasing power over time.

Savings accounts and CDs may not grab headlines, but they're the quiet heroes of personal finance. They provide security, stability, and reliable returns, making them essential tools for any financial plan. Whether you're building an emergency fund, saving for a short-term goal, or looking for a safe place to park your cash, these options ensure your money works as hard as you do. With the variety of providers and rates available, it's never been easier to find an account or CD that fits your needs and budget.

Find these and others resources at this website: www.nextgensage.com/resources

Gold and Silver – Timeless Investments

Gold and silver have captured human imagination for centuries, adorning ancient treasures and serving as symbols of wealth and power. But their value goes beyond aesthetics. These precious metals are among the oldest forms of investment, offering stability and a hedge against inflation in uncertain times. While they won't deliver the explosive growth of stocks or crypto, gold and silver play a unique role in a diversified portfolio, combining tangibility with long-term reliability.

Why Gold and Silver?

When the economy wobbles, investors often flock to gold and silver as a safe haven. Unlike stocks or real estate, their value isn't tied to corporate earnings or local markets. Precious metals derive their worth from scarcity and their universal appeal as a store of value. Whether it's geopolitical turmoil, inflationary pressures, or market volatility, gold and silver tend to hold their ground—or even gain—when other assets falter.

Gold is often viewed as the ultimate hedge against inflation. When the value of paper currency erodes, gold tends to shine, retaining its purchasing power over the long term. Silver, while sometimes overshadowed by gold, offers its own unique appeal. It's more affordable per ounce, making it accessible to smaller investors, and its value is driven by both its role as a precious metal and its industrial applications in electronics, solar panels, and other technologies.

How to Invest in Gold and Silver

There are several ways to invest in gold and silver, depending on your goals, budget, and comfort level:

- **Physical Metals**: Buying bullion coins, bars, or even jewelry is the most straightforward way to own gold and silver. Popular options include American Gold Eagles, Canadian Maple Leafs, and silver bars in various weights. While holding physical metals gives you direct ownership, you'll need to consider storage and security costs.

- **Precious Metal ETFs**: Exchange-traded funds (ETFs) like SPDR Gold Shares (GLD) or iShares Silver Trust (SLV) offer an easy way to gain exposure to gold and silver without handling the physical metal. These funds track the price of the metals and trade on stock exchanges, making them highly liquid and accessible.

- **Mining Stocks**: Investing in companies that mine gold and silver is another option. These stocks often amplify the price movements of the metals, offering higher potential returns—but also higher risks.

- **Futures and Options**: For more experienced investors, trading futures or options contracts on gold and silver can provide leverage and the opportunity for significant gains. However, these strategies come with complexity and high risk.

- **Digital Gold**: Some platforms allow you to purchase fractional amounts of gold and silver stored in secure vaults. This option combines the convenience of ETFs with the tangibility of owning physical metals.

Feature	Physical Gold/Silver	Paper-Based (ETFs/Digital Metals)
Ownership	You own the physical metal	You own shares or digital certificates
Storage	Requires safe storage (home, vaults)	No storage required
Liquidity	Can be sold, but takes more effort	Highly liquid; sell instantly on markets
Costs	Higher premiums, storage fees	Lower fees, but includes management costs
Security	Tangible; no counterparty risk	Risk of issuer default or technical issues
Price Volatility	Directly tied to spot prices	Closely tracks spot prices
Practical Use	Can be used in emergencies (e.g., trade)	Cannot be used directly as money
Minimum Investment	Higher for gold; lower for silver	Fractional ownership available
Accessibility	Local dealers, online shops	Buy through apps or brokerage accounts

Figure 7: Properties of Ownership of Gold/Silver - Physical versus Digital

Gold vs. Silver: Understanding the Differences

Gold and silver are both valuable precious metals, but they serve different roles in an investment portfolio. Gold is often seen as the ultimate safe-haven asset, providing stability during economic uncertainty, inflation, or currency devaluation. It tends to hold its value better over time and is favored by investors looking to preserve wealth. However, gold's higher price per ounce makes it less accessible for small investors. On the other hand, silver is more affordable and accessible, making it an excellent choice for beginners. Silver also has industrial applications in electronics, solar panels, and medical devices, which can influence its price based on industrial demand. While gold is less volatile, silver tends to experience sharper price swings, offering both risk and potential reward for investors. Together, gold and silver can complement each other, with gold offering stability and silver providing growth potential.

Rates of Return

Gold and silver don't generate income like stocks or bonds; instead, their return comes from price appreciation. Historically, gold has delivered long-term returns of around 6-8% annually, depending on the time frame. Silver is more volatile, often experiencing sharper price swings, but its returns can outpace gold during bullish periods.

Unlike other investments, the value of gold and silver doesn't grow consistently year over year. Instead, their performance is often tied to macroeconomic factors, like inflation rates, currency fluctuations, and geopolitical events. For example, during times of financial crisis or high inflation, gold has historically performed well, protecting investors from market declines.

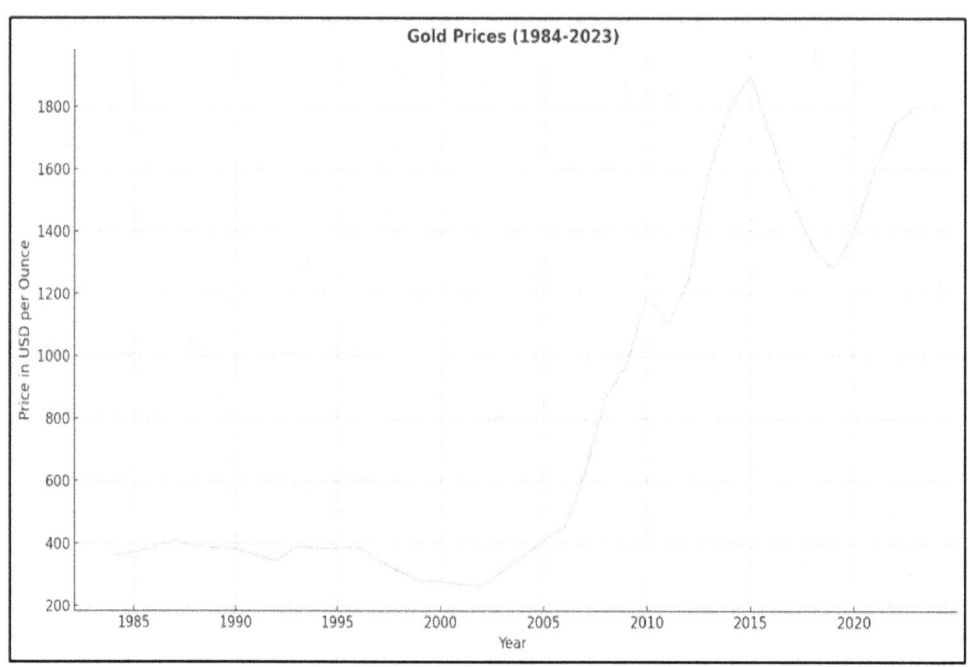

Figure 8: Gold Prices 1984-2023

Capital Requirements

Investing in gold and silver can accommodate a wide range of budgets. Physical coins or bars can be purchased for as little as $30 to $50 for small silver coins or $2,600 or more for a one-ounce gold coin, depending on current prices. ETFs and digital gold platforms often have no minimums, allowing you to start with as little as $100. Mining stocks and futures contracts may require larger investments and come with additional risk.

Risk Factors

While gold and silver are considered safer investments, they're not without risks:

1. **Price Volatility**: Despite their reputation as safe havens, gold and silver prices can be unpredictable, especially over shorter time frames. Silver, in particular, tends to be more volatile than gold due to its industrial demand.
2. **Storage and Security Costs**: If you're buying physical metals, you'll need a secure place to store them, which may involve additional expenses for safes, vaults, or insurance.

3. **Lack of Income**: Precious metals don't generate dividends or interest, which means their value depends entirely on price appreciation. This can make them less attractive during periods of low inflation or stable markets.

4. **Counterparty Risk (ETFs and Digital Gold)**: If you invest in ETFs or digital gold platforms, you're relying on third parties to manage and store your assets. This introduces the potential for mismanagement or fraud.

Method	Description	Minimum Cost	Where to Transact
Physical Gold (Coins/Bars)	Purchase gold coins or small bars from dealers or online platforms. Requires secure storage.	$100 or more, depending on size and weight.	JM Bullion, APMEX, or other reputable dealers.
Gold ETFs	Invest in exchange-traded funds that track the price of gold, such as SPDR Gold Shares (GLD).	No minimum; depends on ETF share price although fractional shares may be available.	Fidelity, Schwab, or Robinhood.
Gold Mining Stocks	Buy stocks in gold mining companies, providing exposure to gold price movements.	$100 or more, depending on stock price.	E*TRADE, Charles Schwab, or other brokerages.
Digital Gold Platforms	Use platforms like Vaulted or OneGold to buy fractional amounts of gold stored in secure vaults.	$10 or more.	Vaulted, OneGold, or Goldmoney.
Gold Jewelry	Buy gold jewelry, though its value is often tied to craftsmanship, not just gold content.	$100 or more; depends on craftsmanship.	Jewelry stores or online marketplaces like Etsy.

Figure 9: Where to Buy/Sell Gold and Silver

Risk Scale: 1 to 2

On the Risk Scale, gold and silver rank between 1 and 2. While their value is stable over the long term, short-term price swings and the lack of income can make them less appealing for certain investors. They're best used as a hedge or a small part of a diversified portfolio rather than the centerpiece of your investment strategy.

Gold and silver may not make headlines the way stocks or cryptocurrencies do, but they're timeless for a reason. They offer stability, act as a hedge against inflation, and provide diversification in any portfolio. Whether you're just starting your investing journey or looking to add a touch of reliability to your holdings, these precious metals remain a steadfast choice in an ever-changing financial landscape.

Investing in Yourself – Turning $100 into Opportunity

When it comes to investments, nothing delivers a better return than betting on yourself. While stocks, bonds, and even gold have their merits, they all rely on external factors like market conditions or company performance. But investing in yourself? That's all about leveraging your own potential. And one of the most powerful ways to see a real, measurable return on a small cash investment is by starting a side hustle or tapping into the gig economy.

With just $100—or sometimes even less—you can plant the seeds for an income stream that grows with your effort. Whether you're driving for a rideshare company, selling handmade crafts, or turning a skill into a freelance business, the opportunities to transform a small investment into something meaningful are nearly endless.

The Gig Economy: Flexible Ways to Start Earning

The gig economy is the ultimate side hustle playground. It's flexible, accessible, and doesn't require a hefty upfront investment. Here are some of the most popular options for getting started:

1. Rideshare Driving (Uber, Lyft)

If you have a car, a valid license, and a clean driving record, you can turn your spare time into cash by driving for companies like Uber or Lyft. The upfront cost? Maybe a tank of gas, some car cleaning supplies, and ensuring your vehicle meets the platform's standards. With demand often spiking during evenings, weekends, and events, rideshare driving can quickly become a lucrative side gig.

2. Delivery Services (DoorDash, Instacart, Uber Eats)

Prefer delivering food or groceries instead of ferrying passengers around? Services like DoorDash, Instacart, and Uber Eats make it easy to start earning without needing much more than a reliable vehicle or even a bicycle in some areas. The flexibility is unbeatable—work as little or as much as you like.

3. Task-Based Platforms (TaskRabbit, Fiverr)

Are you handy around the house or great at assembling furniture? TaskRabbit connects you with people willing to pay for help with everything from fixing leaky faucets to running errands. On the digital side, Fiverr lets you monetize skills like graphic design, writing, or social media management. The only investment here might be a small fee to sign up and perhaps a few tools or supplies for in-person tasks.

4. Pet Sitting and Dog Walking (Rover, Wag)

Love animals? Apps like Rover and Wag connect you with pet owners in need of walkers, sitters, or overnight care. All you need is a little time, a love for furry friends, and maybe some basic pet-care supplies to get started.

5. Renting Out Assets (Turo, Airbnb)

Have a car you're not using all the time? List it on Turo and make money renting it out. Have a spare room or property? Airbnb can turn it into a revenue generator with minimal upfront costs for cleaning, decorating, or marketing your listing.

Side Hustles: Turning Skills and Hobbies into Income

If the gig economy is about flexibility, side hustles are about creativity. They give you the chance to build something truly your own—something that grows as you put time and energy into it. Here are some great ideas to explore:

1. Craft Businesses and Etsy Shops

Are you good with your hands? Whether it's making jewelry, candles, or custom artwork, platforms like Etsy provide an audience for your creations. The $100 investment can go toward buying initial materials or setting up a simple website to showcase your work. As your shop grows, you can reinvest your profits to expand your inventory and reach.

2. Freelancing

Turn a skill into a service. Whether you're a talented writer, photographer, or programmer, platforms like Upwork and Fiverr connect you with clients looking for your expertise. Your investment might include a few dollars for profile enhancements or portfolio samples, but the earning potential is almost limitless.

3. Print-on-Demand Shops (Redbubble, Teespring)

Even if you don't consider yourself an artist, you can create designs for t-shirts, mugs, and tote bags with free or inexpensive design tools like Canva. Print-on-demand platforms like Redbubble and Teespring handle the production and shipping, so all you need to do is upload your designs and promote your store.

4. Social Media Content Creation

If you have a knack for social media, consider starting a YouTube channel, TikTok account, or Instagram page focused on a niche you love—anything from fitness tips to cooking hacks. Your initial investment might be a decent smartphone mount or some basic lighting equipment, but as your audience grows, so do your monetization opportunities through ads, sponsorships, and product placements.

5. Blogging and Affiliate Marketing

Start a blog around a topic you're passionate about—like travel, parenting, or finance. For under $100, you can buy a domain, set up a hosting plan, and start creating content. Once you've built an audience, affiliate marketing (where you earn commissions by promoting products) can generate steady income.

Crafting a Business Around Your Passion

Some of the best side hustles stem from hobbies or passions. Love baking? Start selling homemade cookies or cakes locally. Obsessed with photography? Offer affordable portrait sessions to friends and family. Good at fixing things? Start a handyman business with minimal upfront costs for basic tools.

Here's an example: Let's say you love making scented candles. With $100, you buy wax, wicks, and fragrance oils. You start small, selling to friends and family or at local markets. Over time, you build a loyal customer base and expand to selling on Etsy or through a dedicated website.

That initial $100 could grow into a profitable business with a little effort and creativity.

Why Side Hustles Are So Powerful

Side hustles do more than just put extra cash in your pocket—they teach you valuable skills like marketing, budgeting, and time management. They also give you control over your earning potential. Unlike a traditional job where your income is fixed, a successful side hustle can grow exponentially as you scale your efforts.

For example, driving for Uber might start as a way to make an extra $200 a week, but as you learn the best times and places to drive, you could boost that number significantly. Similarly, an Etsy shop might start as a hobby but turn into a full-fledged business as your products gain popularity.

Mapping Out a Plan to Find the Right Side Hustle

Finding the right side hustle starts with understanding your strengths, interests, and goals. It's about aligning what you enjoy and what you're good at with opportunities that can make you money. Before jumping into the first idea that comes your way, take time to map out a plan: What are your skills? How much time can you realistically commit? Do you need something low-cost to start, or can you invest a little upfront? By answering these questions, you'll be able to choose a side hustle that fits your lifestyle and goals, ensuring it's not just profitable but also sustainable and enjoyable. Remember, the best side hustle is one that excites you and moves you closer to your version of financial freedom.

Questionnaire: Finding the Right Side Hustle for You

Answer the following questions to help identify a side hustle that fits your life and goals:

1. **What are your strengths?**
    - ☐ Creative (e.g., design, writing)
    - ☐ Technical (e.g., coding, problem-solving)
    - ☐ People-oriented (e.g., sales, customer service)
    - ☐ Hands-on (e.g., crafting, building)
1. **How much time can you dedicate to a side hustle each week?**
    - ☐ 5-10 hours
    - ☐ 10-20+ hours
    - ☐ Weekends

- ☐ Nights

1. **What's your starting budget?**

- ☐ $0–$50 (no upfront costs)
- ☐ $50–$100 (low investment)
- ☐ $100+ (willing to invest more)

1. **What's your main goal for starting a side hustle?**

- ☐ Extra income for daily expenses
- ☐ Saving for a specific goal (e.g., trip, home)
- ☐ Building skills for future opportunities
- ☐ Creating a long-term business

1. **What kinds of tasks do you enjoy most?**

- ☐ Working with people (e.g., tutoring, coaching)
- ☐ Solo work (e.g., freelancing, blogging)
- ☐ Hands-on projects (e.g., crafts, reselling)
- ☐ Online tasks (e.g., virtual assistant, content creation)

Putting It All Together

Once you've answered the questionnaire, look for overlap: What are you good at? What excites you? What fits into your current schedule and budget? Use these answers to brainstorm side hustle ideas that make sense for you. Whether it's selling handmade products, freelancing online, or offering a service in your local community, the right side hustle is out there—you just need to find it and take that first step.

Meet Lisa: From Weekend Baker to Business Owner

Lisa, a 32-year-old marketing assistant, loved baking in her free time. Friends and family often raved about her cakes and pastries, but she never thought of it as more than a hobby. One day, after setting a goal to invest more for her future, Lisa realized she needed extra income to make it happen. With just **$100** for ingredients and supplies, she decided to turn her passion into a small weekend side hustle: baking custom cakes for birthdays and special occasions.

At first, Lisa started small—posting photos of her creations on social media and offering her cakes to local friends and coworkers. Word spread quickly, and soon she was baking three or four cakes a week. After covering her costs, Lisa was making an extra $200 to $300 a month—money she immediately started investing into a retirement account and an emergency fund. Over time, her baking skills improved, and her customer base grew as people began recommending her to friends and family.

Within a year, Lisa had a steady stream of orders and enough demand to consider expanding her hustle. She created a simple website, streamlined her baking process, and increased her prices as her cakes became known for their quality and design. What started as a way to fund her investments turned into a thriving side business. Now, Lisa is planning to leave her 9-to-5 job to turn her baking hustle into a full-time business—one that not only supports her financially but also brings her joy and a sense of purpose.

The Lesson

Lisa's story shows that a side hustle doesn't have to stay small. By starting with something you're good at and passionate about, you can create a reliable income stream. That extra money can help fund your investments, savings, or goals, and who knows—like Lisa, you might even discover a path to a full-time business doing something you love.

The Risk Scale: 1 to 3

Most gig economy jobs rank at a **1** on the risk scale—there's little upfront investment, and the main risk is your time. Side hustles that require a bit more investment, like setting up an Etsy shop or starting a business, might rank closer to a **3** due to the effort and creativity involved. But the potential rewards make them well worth it.

Final Thoughts

Investing in yourself through side hustles and gig work isn't just about earning extra money—it's about planting seeds for growth and opportunity. With just $100 and a spark of determination, you're not only creating an additional income stream but also building valuable skills, expanding your network, and unlocking your potential. These experiences can lead to new opportunities, open unexpected doors, and foster a sense of pride that goes far beyond a paycheck.

Every small effort you put in today—whether it's delivering groceries, designing handmade jewelry, freelancing, or starting a blog—compounds over time, just like financial investments. The skills you learn, the connections you make, and the confidence you gain become assets that will serve you for years to come. More importantly, investing in yourself allows you to take control of your future, proving that you don't need a huge budget to make a big impact on your life.

So, start where you are, with what you have. That little side hustle you begin today could be the spark that lights the way to your financial independence. Remember: the best investment you will ever make is in yourself, because the returns are truly limitless. Believe in your ideas, take action, and keep moving forward—because your future self will thank you for the steps you take today.

Real Estate – Building Wealth Brick by Brick

Real estate is the classic dream investment. Who hasn't fantasized about owning a few rental properties, watching the rent checks roll in, and retiring early with a portfolio of bricks and mortar? While it may seem out of reach for someone starting with $100, real estate offers more opportunities for entry than you might think. Whether it's through fractional ownership, creative strategies, or side hustles that lead to property investments, this chapter explores how real estate can become a key part of your wealth-building strategy.

The Case for Real Estate

Why is real estate such a revered investment? For one, it's tangible—you can see it, touch it, and maybe even live in it. Unlike stocks or bonds, real estate serves a dual purpose: it can generate income through rent while appreciating in value over time. It's a time-tested hedge against inflation and provides the kind of stability that appeals to both seasoned investors and beginners.

"Buy land, they're not making it anymore." Mark Twain

But real estate isn't just about buying a house or a rental property. These days, there are innovative ways to get involved, even if you're starting small. Whether it's crowdfunding, REITs, or flipping a spare room into a money-maker, you can dip your toes into the real estate market with much less capital than you think.

The Power of Home Ownership: Building Wealth Over Time

Homeownership has long been a cornerstone of the American Dream, offering more than just a place to live. It provides stability, pride, and one of the most effective ways to build wealth over time. Unlike renting, where monthly payments benefit a landlord, owning a home allows you to turn housing expenses into equity. Each mortgage payment increases your stake in the property, effectively turning your monthly bills into a form of forced savings. Over time, homes also tend to appreciate in value. Historical data shows that in many markets, home values rise at an average annual rate of 3-5%, making homeownership an excellent long-term investment.

The financial benefits don't stop there. Homeownership often comes with significant tax advantages, such as deductions for mortgage interest and property taxes, which can reduce your overall tax burden. For those looking to maximize their investment, renting out part of a home, such as a basement apartment, can provide additional income while offsetting the costs of ownership.

However, homeownership isn't without challenges. Maintenance, repairs, and property taxes can add up, and market downturns may temporarily reduce home values. Yet, for those willing to take a long-term view, owning a home remains one of the most accessible and rewarding paths to financial security.

Home Ownership Example: The Journey of Jake and Emily

Jake and Emily, a married couple in their late 20s, purchased their first home in 2003. It was a modest three-bedroom house in a suburban neighborhood, priced at $200,000. With a 20% down payment of $40,000 and a 30-year fixed mortgage at a 5% interest rate, their monthly mortgage payment (excluding taxes and insurance) came to around $860. The couple viewed the home as both a place to start their family and a way to build long-term financial security.

Over the years, Jake and Emily diligently made their monthly payments, gradually building equity in their home. They also invested in modest upgrades, like renovating the kitchen and landscaping the backyard, which not only made the home more enjoyable but also increased its value. Meanwhile, the neighborhood grew in popularity, with new schools, parks, and shopping centers driving demand for housing in the area.

By 2023, 20 years later, the value of their home had appreciated significantly, reaching $450,000, thanks to a combination of market growth and their improvements.

Over the same period, Jake and Emily had paid off a substantial portion of their mortgage, reducing their loan balance to just $60,000. This meant they now had $390,000 in equity—a dramatic increase from their initial $40,000 down payment.

The financial benefits didn't stop there. By owning their home, Jake and Emily avoided rising rental costs, which would have totaled over $250,000 across 20 years. They also enjoyed tax savings from deducting mortgage interest and property taxes during the earlier years of their loan. As they approached retirement, the couple planned to downsize to a smaller home, using their equity to pay for it outright, leaving them mortgage-free with a significant nest egg.

Their story highlights how homeownership, combined with time and market growth, can create substantial wealth. Starting with a modest investment, Jake and Emily not only provided a stable home for their family but also built an asset that secured their financial future.

Saving Toward Home Ownership

For those dreaming of owning property outright, patience, persistence, and a clear strategy are the keys to success.

While $100 won't buy you a duplex today, it can be the start of something much bigger. By taking small but consistent steps, you can steadily work your way toward the ultimate goal of property ownership.

One possible step is to start a real estate fund. Open a separate savings or investment account dedicated solely to building capital for your real estate goals. Treat this account as sacred—money deposited here is for your future property, not everyday expenses. Even modest contributions of $100 a month can grow significantly over time, especially if placed in an interest-bearing savings account, index fund, or other low-risk investments. The consistency matters more than the amount; as the balance grows, so will your motivation to keep saving.

To accelerate your journey, take advantage of down payment assistance programs. Many state and local governments, as well as nonprofits, offer grants or low-interest loans specifically designed to help first-time homebuyers. These programs can reduce the financial burden of a down payment, allowing you to purchase a home much sooner than if you were relying on savings alone. While these programs often come with income limits or specific requirements, they can be a game-changer for aspiring homeowners with limited capital.

For buyers looking to stretch their savings even further, FHA loans can make property ownership far more accessible. Backed by the Federal Housing Administration, these loans allow qualified buyers to purchase a home with as little as 3.5% down—significantly less than the 20% typically required for conventional loans. FHA loans are particularly valuable for first-time buyers who may not have a large amount of cash saved but have steady income and a manageable credit profile. By lowering the barriers to entry, these loans open the door to property ownership for those willing to take the first step.

While the road to property ownership may seem long, each of these strategies—saving consistently, leveraging assistance programs, and exploring flexible loan options—brings you closer to the goal. Owning real estate isn't just about having a place to call your own; it's about creating an asset that grows in value, builds wealth, and provides opportunities for financial independence. Every small step you take today lays the foundation for a future where owning property becomes a reality.

Residential Mortgage Loans

A residential mortgage loan is a tool that allows individuals to purchase a home by borrowing money from a lender while spreading the repayment over a set period—typically 15, 20, or 30 years. Mortgages make homeownership more accessible by reducing the need for a large upfront payment. These loans are offered by traditional banks, credit unions, mortgage lenders, and online platforms like Rocket Mortgage, Better.com, and local credit unions, providing a variety of options to suit different financial needs.

Basic Criteria to Qualify for a Residential Mortgage:

- **Credit Score**: Generally, a score of 620 or higher is needed for conventional loans. FHA loans may accept lower scores.
- **Loan-to-Value Ratio (LTV)**: Lenders typically require a down payment of 5–20% of the home's value, meaning the loan covers 80–95% of the purchase price.
- **Debt-to-Income Ratio (DTI)**: Most lenders prefer a DTI of 36% or lower, though some allow up to 43% with compensating factors.

- **Stable Income**: Borrowers must show proof of steady income through pay stubs, tax returns, or bank statements.
- **Savings for Closing Costs**: Beyond the down payment, expect to pay 2–5% of the home price for closing costs, including fees for appraisals, loan origination, and legal services.

By understanding these key factors and shopping around, buyers can secure a mortgage that fits their budget and financial goals. Lenders like Wells Fargo, Quicken Loans, and local credit unions often provide personalized options, making it easier to take that first step toward homeownership.

Mortgage Insurance for Low-Down-Payment Loans

When a borrower puts down less than 20% on a home, most lenders require mortgage insurance to protect against default. For conventional loans, this comes in the form of Private Mortgage Insurance (PMI), which typically costs 0.5% to 1% of the loan amount annually. For government-backed loans like FHA loans, mortgage insurance premiums (MIP) are required upfront and as part of monthly payments. While mortgage insurance adds to the cost of homeownership, it enables buyers to qualify for a mortgage with as little as 3-5% down, making homeownership accessible sooner. Once the borrower's equity reaches 20%, PMI can often be canceled, reducing monthly costs.

Understanding the Risks of Homeownership

Homeownership is often viewed as a reliable way to build wealth and achieve financial stability, but it comes with its own set of challenges and risks. One of the most significant factors to consider is market volatility. While home values have historically appreciated over the long term, short-term fluctuations can occur due to economic downturns, changes in the local housing market, or rising interest rates. For homeowners looking to sell during a market downturn, the property's value may temporarily drop, resulting in a loss or a lower-than-expected return. This risk emphasizes the importance of viewing homeownership as a long-term investment rather than a quick opportunity for profit.

Another key challenge is the ongoing financial responsibility that comes with owning a home. Beyond mortgage payments, homeowners must budget for property taxes, insurance, maintenance, and unexpected repairs. Be careful not to buy that ticket to the "Home Repair Carnival" where the rides are expensive and there is no exit. A leaking roof, broken furnace, or foundation issue can quickly add thousands of dollars in expenses, requiring homeowners to have an emergency fund or other financial safeguards in place. Additionally, homeownership ties up a significant amount of capital in an illiquid asset. Unlike stocks or bonds, which can be sold relatively quickly, selling a home takes time, and the process can be complicated if you need cash urgently.

While these risks are real, they can be managed through careful planning and financial preparedness. By understanding the full scope of homeownership responsibilities, buyers can make informed decisions and enjoy the many benefits of owning a home over the long term.

Residential Development and Re-Development: Creating Value

Residential development and re-development offer unique opportunities to create significant value while addressing the housing needs of growing communities. Development involves building new homes or multi-family units in areas with high demand, while re-development focuses on revitalizing older properties. Both approaches can transform neighborhoods and provide substantial financial returns for investors.

Re-development, in particular, has gained popularity as investors look to purchase underperforming properties and renovate them for modern use. Urban revitalization projects often breathe new life into communities, turning run-down buildings into desirable homes or apartments. Savvy investors may also take advantage of zoning changes to convert single-family lots into multi-family developments, increasing density and profitability. Additionally, incorporating sustainable upgrades like solar panels or energy-efficient systems can attract buyers willing to pay a premium.

For example, a developer purchasing an old six-unit apartment building for $400,000 in an up-and-coming neighborhood might spend $200,000 on renovations. By increasing rents by 50%, they could raise the property's value to $850,000, creating $250,000 in equity. While development and re-development come with risks like construction delays or budget overruns, careful planning and market analysis can make these strategies highly lucrative.

By exploring these avenues—homeownership, commercial real estate, or residential development—you can leverage real estate's power to build wealth, create opportunities, and make a lasting financial impact.

Financing Home Construction

Building your own home offers the unique opportunity to design a space perfectly suited to your needs. However, financing the construction process differs significantly from obtaining a traditional mortgage for an existing property. Construction loans are tailored specifically for this purpose, covering expenses like materials, labor, permits, and even land acquisition. These loans are typically short-term, designed to fund the construction phase, and are later converted into a standard mortgage or paid off entirely.

Construction loans come with distinct requirements that reflect the added risks associated with home building. Borrowers need to demonstrate financial stability, provide a detailed plan, and meet the following criteria:

- **Strong Credit Score**: A credit score of 700 or higher is typically required.
- **Detailed Construction Plan**: Borrowers must present comprehensive plans, including blueprints, budgets, timelines, and a contract with a licensed builder.
- **Down Payment**: Lenders generally require a 20–25% down payment due to the higher risk involved.
- **Debt-to-Income Ratio (DTI)**: A DTI of 45% or lower is preferred to ensure borrowers can manage the loan and other financial obligations.
- **Land Ownership**: If the borrower already owns the land, it can serve as equity for the loan.
- **Interest Reserves**: Many construction loans include interest reserves to cover payments during the building phase.

Borrowers can choose between different types of construction loans depending on their needs. Construction-to-permanent loans transition into a traditional mortgage once construction is complete, eliminating the need for refinancing. Alternatively, stand-alone construction loans are short-term loans that must be refinanced or paid off after the building phase ends. Both options have their advantages, and the right choice depends on the borrower's financial situation and long-term goals.

Several types of lenders provide construction financing. Large banks like Wells Fargo, Chase, and Bank of America are known for their competitive terms and reliable services. Local banks and credit unions often provide more flexible options and a deeper understanding of the regional market, making them ideal for custom or unique projects. Specialized lenders like BuildLoan focus exclusively on construction loans and offer tailored services for borrowers and homebuilders. For a streamlined application process, online platforms such as LendingTree and SoFi allow borrowers to compare rates and terms quickly.

While construction loans require more planning and higher qualifications than traditional mortgages, they offer the ability to create a home designed specifically for your needs. With careful preparation and the right lending partner, financing a custom-built home can be a smooth and rewarding process.

Commercial Real Estate: Opportunities Across Sectors

For investors seeking steady income and long-term growth, commercial real estate offers a world of opportunities. From apartment buildings and retail spaces to warehouses and office buildings, commercial properties cater to a wide range of financial goals and risk tolerances. Multi-family apartment complexes, for instance, are a popular choice for those looking to generate reliable income, as demand for affordable rental housing remains strong in most markets. Investors can further increase the value of these properties through renovations or upgrades, enabling them to charge higher rents.

Retail spaces, while facing challenges from the rise of e-commerce, can still be lucrative if located in high-traffic areas or leased to strong, stable tenants. Similarly, warehouses and industrial spaces are in high demand thanks to the booming logistics and e-commerce industries. These properties often come with long-term tenants, providing investors with stable cash flow. Office buildings, while influenced by trends like remote work, continue to offer strong returns in prime locations with high occupancy rates.

Commercial real estate provides several advantages. Higher returns, long-term leases, and diversification make it an appealing addition to an investment portfolio. For example, an investor purchasing a $500,000 retail strip center with three tenants could generate $60,000 in annual rent. After accounting for expenses, they earn an 8% annual return—and with lease renewals or rent increases, their income continues to grow over time. While commercial real estate often requires significant upfront capital and active management, the rewards can be well worth the effort.

Keep in mind that this section provides an only brief overview of commercial real estate, touching on its diverse opportunities and potential for income and growth. However, investing in commercial properties requires in-depth market analysis, a solid understanding of property management, and familiarity with commercial finance markets. Each sector—whether apartments, retail, office, or industrial—comes with its own unique dynamics and challenges that demand careful evaluation. This book serves as an introduction to the asset class, offering a foundation for understanding its potential, but aspiring investors should conduct thorough research and seek professional advice before delving into larger, more complex commercial real estate ventures.

Understanding the Risks of Rental Properties

Investing in rental properties can provide a steady stream of income and long-term wealth, but it also comes with unique risks and challenges that require careful consideration. One of the most significant risks is management challenges. Rental properties require ongoing attention, from finding and screening tenants to handling day-to-day maintenance and repairs. A vacant unit can quickly turn from an income-producing asset into a financial drain, leaving the owner responsible for mortgage payments, taxes, and utilities without rental income to offset costs. Additionally, unexpected tenant issues, such as late payments or property damage, can add stress and financial strain.

Another challenge with rental properties is market risk. Rent prices and property values are heavily influenced by economic conditions, local demand, and competition. In an economic downturn, tenants may struggle to pay rent, leading to higher vacancy rates or the need to reduce rental prices to stay competitive. Property values can also fluctuate, making it challenging to sell the property at a profit during unfavorable market conditions. Investors need to be prepared for these potential setbacks and have a financial cushion to cover periods of lower cash flow.

Finally, rental properties require time and expertise. While hiring a property management company can alleviate some of the responsibilities, it adds to the overall costs, reducing profitability. For investors managing their own properties, the workload can be significant, particularly if they own multiple units or properties in different locations.

Despite these challenges, rental properties remain a powerful investment tool when approached with a solid strategy. Investors who plan ahead, budget for maintenance and vacancies, and take a hands-on approach to management can mitigate these risks and enjoy the benefits of steady income, property appreciation, and portfolio diversification.

Real Estate Syndication: Teaming Up for Big Opportunities

For those ready to step into larger real estate opportunities without buying an entire property themselves, real estate syndication offers a powerful way to invest in high-value projects. Syndication pools money from multiple investors to purchase commercial properties, apartment complexes, or other large-scale developments, allowing participants to share in the returns without the hassle of managing the property. Platforms like RealtyMogul specialize in these types of investments, catering primarily to accredited investors—individuals who meet certain income or net worth thresholds. With minimum investments typically starting around $5,000, syndication provides access to deals that would otherwise be out of reach for individual investors, delivering returns through rental income and property appreciation. While the barrier to entry is higher, syndication offers a more passive investment option for those looking to diversify into premium real estate without taking on full ownership responsibilities.

Getting Started: Real Estate Options for $100

Real estate may seem like an unattainable investment for those with limited funds, but today's market offers several ways to get started with as little as $100. By leveraging innovative platforms and creative strategies, you can begin building a real estate portfolio without the need for substantial capital.

One of the most accessible options is Real Estate Investment Trusts (REITs), which allow you to invest in income-generating properties like apartment buildings, office spaces, and shopping malls through the stock market. With REITs, you're essentially buying shares in a company that owns and manages real estate. The beauty of REITs is that you can start with the cost of a single share, often less than $100, through brokerages like Fidelity or Robinhood. These investments not only offer exposure to diversified real estate portfolios but also generate passive income through dividends. Historically, REITs have delivered average annual returns of 8–10%, making them an attractive option for beginner investors.

For those interested in a more hands-on approach, crowdfunding platforms have opened the door to property investment for small investors. Platforms like Fundrise and Roofstock let you pool your money with others to fund real estate projects such as commercial developments or rental units. With minimum investments starting as low as $10, these platforms democratize access to real estate, offering returns that typically range from 6–12%, depending on the type of project and its risk level. Crowdfunding provides a unique opportunity to participate in larger projects without needing to manage properties yourself.

Another creative option is house hacking, which turns your primary residence into an income-generating asset. House hacking is when you rent out part of your home to offset your mortgage. It's like having roommates, but instead of sharing your Netflix password, you're sharing your living space for profit. This strategy could involve renting out a spare room on Airbnb, leasing your basement to a long-term tenant, or even converting a garage into a rental unit. House hacking allows you to offset your mortgage or housing expenses while building equity in your property. If you already own your home, $100 might go toward cleaning, decorating, or listing fees to get started. The rental income generated can significantly reduce your monthly expenses, providing both financial relief and investment benefits.

For those drawn to land ownership, land flipping and leasing offers a surprising entry point. Websites like AcreTrader and Landmodo allow you to purchase small plots of land with minimal upfront investment—often as low as $50. Whether you hold the land to sell later at a higher value or lease it for purposes like agriculture or parking, land ownership can provide a unique and potentially profitable real estate venture. While returns vary, land values generally appreciate over time, adding another layer of potential growth.

Finally, real estate side hustles can help you earn and save the money needed for larger investments. While you may not be able to buy a property outright with $100, you can leverage your time and skills to build capital and industry knowledge. Offering property management services, cleaning or maintenance for landlords, or even becoming a licensed real estate agent are excellent ways to break into the industry. These side hustles not only generate extra income but also connect you with valuable networks and provide insights that can accelerate your real estate journey.

Whether you're investing in REITs, exploring crowdfunding, or turning your spare room into a rental, these strategies show that you don't need to wait for a windfall to start building wealth through real estate. With creativity and determination, $100 can be the first step toward a rewarding investment future.

Option	What It Is	Starting Cost	Potential Returns	Key Benefits
REITs	Invest in companies that own/manage real estate	Cost of 1 share	8–10% annual returns through dividends	Passive income, easy to access via brokerages
Crowdfunding Platforms	Pool money to fund real estate projects	$10–$100	6–12%, depending on project type	Low-cost entry into larger real estate deals
House Hacking	Rent out part of your primary residence	Minimal costs	Monthly rental income	Offsets mortgage, builds equity
Land Flipping/Leasing	Buy small plots of land for resale or leasing	$50+	Varies; land tends to appreciate	Affordable entry into property ownership
Real Estate Side Hustles	Services like property management or cleaning	Varies; ~$100	Income from services provided	Builds capital, networks, and experience

Figure 10: How to Invest $100 in Real Estate

Commercial Real Estate Financing

Financing for commercial real estate (CRE) allows investors to purchase income-generating properties such as apartment complexes, retail spaces, warehouses, and office buildings. While like residential loans, CRE financing comes with stricter requirements and larger down payments due to the higher perceived risk. Lenders focus heavily on the property's ability to generate income and the borrower's financial qualifications.

Key Criteria for Commercial Real Estate Loans:

- **Loan-to-Value Ratio (LTV)**: Typically, 65-80%, requiring 20-35% as a down payment.
- **Debt Service Coverage Ratio (DSCR)**: Minimum of 1.25, ensuring net operating income exceeds loan payments by at least 25%.
- **Credit Score**: Strong personal or business credit, usually 680 or higher.
- **Income and Cash Flow**: Demonstrated ability of the property to generate sufficient income to cover expenses and debt payments.
- **Property Type and Value**: The condition, location, and income potential of the property are carefully assessed.
- **Experience**: Preference is given to borrowers with prior experience in managing or investing in commercial real estate.

Borrowers can secure CRE loans from traditional banks like Wells Fargo and Chase, credit unions, or online lenders such as LendingTree Commercial and RealtyMogul. For small businesses, government-backed programs like SBA 504 and SBA 7(a) offer attractive financing options with lower down payments. While the process requires more analysis and preparation, CRE loans can provide a pathway to high-value investments and long-term wealth creation.

The Risk Scale: 2 to 4

On our **Risk Scale**, real estate ranks between **2 and 4**, depending on the type of investment. REITs and crowdfunding platforms are on the lower end, offering diversification and liquidity. Owning property outright or engaging in house flipping carries higher risks but also higher rewards.

Final Thoughts

Real estate isn't just about owning properties—it's about finding creative ways to build wealth with the resources you have. Whether you're starting with $100 or saving for a down payment, there are countless ways to get involved in the real estate market and start seeing returns.

From fractional ownership to house hacking, the opportunities are as diverse as the properties themselves. With patience, creativity, and a little hustle, real estate can become a cornerstone of your financial future—brick by brick.

Stock Investments - The Cornerstone of Wealth Creation

The stock market is a cornerstone of modern investing. For decades, it's been the go-to destination for building wealth, generating income, and, for some, chasing adrenaline-fueled gains. Whether you're a beginner with $100 or a seasoned investor managing a portfolio, the stock market offers a world of opportunity. But to truly succeed, you need to understand the tools and strategies available, from long-term investments in stable companies to dividend reinvestment plans (DRIPs) and more advanced approaches like options trading.

This chapter dives into the fundamentals of stock investing, explores the nuances of day trading and options, and highlights how strategies like DRIPs can turn small earnings into long-term wealth.

The Magic of Owning Stocks

When you buy a stock, you're purchasing a piece of a company—your own tiny slice of its success. Stocks represent ownership, and with that comes the potential for two types of rewards: capital appreciation (the stock price going up) and dividends (a share of the company's profits paid out to shareholders). While stocks can be volatile in the short term, they've historically been one of the best-performing asset classes over the long term, offering average annual returns of **8–10%**.

Consider Amazon. Back in 1997, its stock debuted at just $18 per share. Fast forward to today, and those shares—after splits and years of growth—are worth thousands. A $100 investment in Amazon's early days could have turned into a small fortune – over $193,000. While not every stock will perform like Amazon, the stock market offers countless opportunities for those willing to do their homework.

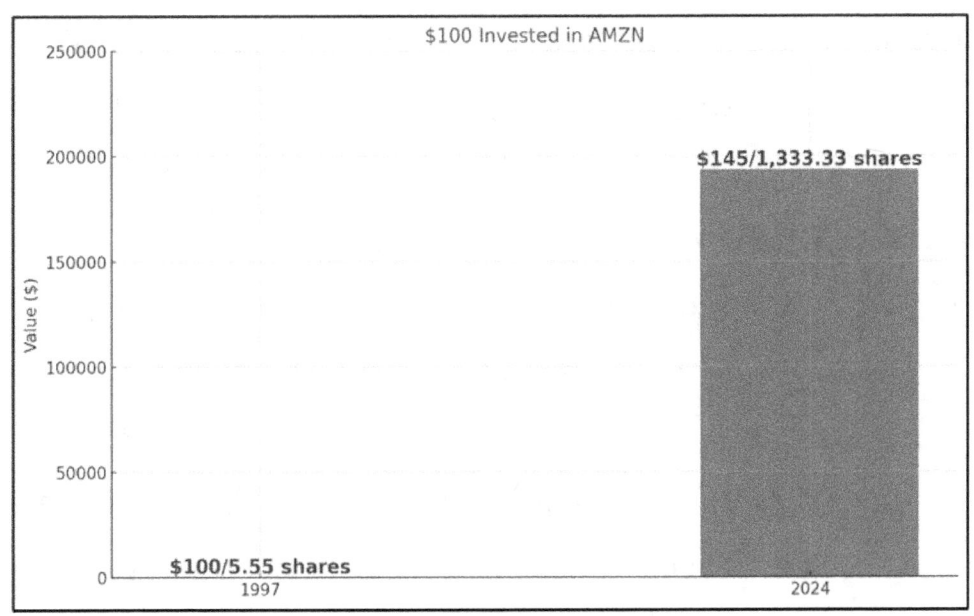

Figure 11: $100 Invested in AMZN in 1997, worth $193,332 in 2024

Selecting the Right Stock

Choosing the right stock can feel overwhelming at first, especially with so many companies to evaluate. However, by focusing on a few key principles and understanding both traditional and modern approaches to stock analysis, the process becomes much more manageable. Successful stock selection starts with aligning investments to your goals, whether you're looking for long-term growth, steady income, or a mix of both.

One of the foundational methods for evaluating stocks is **fundamental analysis**, which focuses on a company's financial health and competitive position. This approach involves examining factors such as earnings growth, profit margins, and debt levels to determine whether a stock is overvalued or undervalued. For example, the Price-to-Earnings (P/E) ratio can provide insight into how a company's share price compares to its earnings, helping investors identify potential opportunities. Beyond the numbers, strong companies often have a proven track record of success, including consistent earnings growth and resilience during economic downturns. Dividend-paying stocks, such as Coca-Cola or Johnson & Johnson, provide an additional layer of appeal for investors seeking reliable income, as these companies tend to generate steady cash flow and reward shareholders over time. Another important aspect of fundamental analysis is identifying businesses with a durable competitive advantage, often referred to as a "moat," which allows them to maintain a strong position in their industry.

While fundamental analysis focuses on the long-term health of a business, **technical analysis** provides a different perspective by looking at stock price movements and trading patterns. Investors who use this method analyze price charts to identify trends, momentum, and opportunities for short-term gains. Patterns like support and resistance levels, moving averages, and trading volume are key indicators that signal whether a stock is experiencing bullish or bearish momentum. For instance, if a stock consistently trades above its 50-day moving average, it may suggest growing investor confidence and upward price potential. Technical analysis also emphasizes market sentiment, using tools such as the Relative Strength Index (RSI) to determine whether a stock is overbought or oversold. This method is particularly useful for short-term traders seeking to capitalize on price movements rather than focusing solely on a company's fundamentals.

In today's investing environment, the influence of social trends cannot be ignored. The rise of the meme stock phenomenon has demonstrated how quickly stocks can surge based on online hype rather than traditional financial metrics. Stocks like GameStop and AMC Entertainment saw meteoric rises driven by retail investors on platforms such as Reddit's WallStreetBets, fueled by viral enthusiasm and a sense of collective action. While some investors made substantial profits, others faced significant losses when the hype dissipated and the stock prices came crashing down. Unlike traditional investing, meme stocks are powered by speculation and crowd sentiment, making them highly volatile and unpredictable. For investors intrigued by these trends, it's essential to approach with caution and understand the inherent risks of trading stocks that are disconnected from their underlying business performance.

Ultimately, selecting the right stock is about balance. Combining fundamental analysis to identify businesses with strong long-term potential, technical analysis to understand price behavior, and awareness of social trends allows investors to make well-informed decisions. The goal is not to chase the most exciting headline but to invest in companies that demonstrate real value, strong financials, and sustainable growth. Successful investors look beyond stock prices and focus on businesses with the potential to thrive over time, while remaining mindful of short-term market dynamics and emerging trends. By staying disciplined and informed, you can navigate the complexities of stock selection with greater confidence.

Fundamental Analysis: The Foundation of Good Investing

Investing without fundamental analysis is like trying to bake a cake without checking if you've got flour in the pantry—it might work out, but odds are, you're setting yourself up for a disaster. Fundamental analysis is all about looking under the hood of a company to see if it's a sleek, reliable sports car or just a shiny clunker with a sputtering engine. This approach focuses on the nitty-gritty: financial health, competitive edge, and whether the company can hold its own in the cutthroat world of business. Think of it as the due diligence that separates smart investing from glorified gambling.

"It's far better to buy a wonderful company at a fair price than a fair company at a wonderful price." Warren Buffet

Let's start with **revenue and earnings**, the bread and butter of any business. Revenue tells you how much money a company brings in, while earnings are what's left after paying the bills (and yes, even giants like Amazon have bills). Ideally, you want a company with a steady upward trend in both. It's like dating—you're looking for someone reliable, not someone who's flush one month and couch-surfing the next. A one-off revenue spike might look impressive, but steady growth over several years shows a company knows how to keep the lights on. Apple is a classic example here: year after year, they rake in billions, and they do it with a swagger that screams, "We've got this."

Now, let's talk about **debt levels**, the financial equivalent of checking if your friend's credit card is maxed out before they book a vacation to Bora Bora. A company with too much debt is walking a financial tightrope, and even a small misstep—like an economic downturn—can send it tumbling. The debt-to-equity ratio is your trusty guide here, showing how much a company relies on borrowed money versus what it actually owns. Low-debt companies are like those folks who pay off their credit card balance every month—they're not flashy, but they're solid. High-debt companies? Think of them as that friend who just leased a Tesla but is still asking to split the bill at dinner.

A company's **competitive advantage** is where things get exciting. This is its "it factor," the secret sauce that keeps competitors awake at night. Maybe it's a killer brand, revolutionary tech, or an army of loyal customers who'd rather lose an arm than switch to a rival. Apple, again, nails this with its ecosystem. The moment you buy an iPhone, you're sucked into a world of AirPods, MacBooks, and iPads—all designed to make you forget the outside world exists. Or take Coca-Cola: their moat is so strong that even people who swear off soda still know the brand's jingle.

Companies with a strong moat can weather storms and thrive when others falter, making them investor gold.

And then there's **management**, the unsung heroes—or villains—of a company's story. Good leadership can turn a solid business into an unstoppable juggernaut, while bad leadership can sink even the best ship. You want forward-thinkers at the helm, people who are playing chess while others are fumbling with checkers. Look at Tesla and Elon Musk (love him or hate him)—he took the electric car from niche curiosity to global phenomenon. Great leaders inspire confidence, adapt to challenges, and know how to steer the company toward growth without crashing into regulatory icebergs.

But wait, there's more! Every **industry** has its quirks, so you've got to adjust your analysis accordingly. In tech, it's all about innovation—who's got the next big thing? In utilities, boring is beautiful; stable earnings and dividends make them the tortoise in the race to wealth. Meanwhile, cyclical industries like energy or auto manufacturing are like roller coasters—wildly profitable in good times but a stomach-churning ride in downturns. Keeping tabs on industry trends, regulations, and disruptions (hello, sustainability!) can help you spot winners and avoid landmines.

To see this in action, let's return to our perennial favorite, Apple. This is a company with a history of robust earnings, a clean balance sheet, and a brand so powerful that people willingly camp outside stores for hours just to buy the latest iPhone. Their competitive advantage? A product ecosystem that's basically a tech cult—once you're in, it's hard to get out. And with a leadership team that seems to have the Midas touch, Apple consistently positions itself for long-term growth while others scramble to keep up.

Fundamental analysis, when done right, is less about predicting the next big thing and more about identifying companies that have what it takes to thrive over the long haul. Sure, stock prices will jump and dip in the short term, but a solid company is like a good friend—they'll stick around when it matters. And who doesn't want a portfolio filled with winners that are built to last?

Fundamental Example: Dividend Growth Investing

Dividend growth investing is a strategy that focuses on building a portfolio of reliable, high-quality companies that consistently reward shareholders with growing dividend payments. It's like finding the friend who always picks up the check—and then ups their generosity every year. These companies tend to have strong revenue and earnings growth, manageable debt levels, and a solid competitive advantage, often reflected in iconic brands, innovative products, or market dominance.

For example, Procter & Gamble fits the bill perfectly. With its household-name brands, steady earnings, and over 65 years of dividend increases, it's the poster child for this approach. Companies like this combine financial resilience with shareholder-friendly policies, making them ideal for investors seeking a mix of income and long-term growth. Plus, their consistent payouts offer peace of mind, even when the market gets choppy.

By reinvesting those growing dividends, investors can benefit from the magic of compounding while enjoying the reliability of steady income—no need to chase the latest market fad when you've got a strategy this solid.

Decoding the Art of Technical Analysis

If fundamental analysis is like getting to know someone's personality and values, technical analysis is more like studying their habits and quirks. It's all about analyzing stock price movements, patterns, and momentum to make predictions about what might happen next. Think of it as interpreting the market's mood swings—a mix of psychology, statistics, and a bit of artistry. For traders, particularly those who thrive on short-term opportunities, technical analysis is a valuable tool for identifying when to buy or sell.

At its core, technical analysis revolves around price charts. These charts are the market's diary, mapping out past movements and hinting at potential future trends. Candlestick charts, for instance, provide detailed snapshots of price action within specific timeframes. Each candlestick reveals whether the market was bullish, bearish, or undecided. Line charts are simpler, showing just the closing prices over time, while bar charts offer more detail by including open, high, low, and close prices. Each type has its place in a trader's toolkit, depending on the story they want to uncover.

The magic happens when patterns start to emerge. Certain shapes and movements on these charts have stood the test of time and are widely regarded as predictors of market behavior. Here are some of the most popular chart patterns and what they indicate:

- Head and Shoulders: This classic pattern signals a reversal. The "head" is a peak flanked by two lower peaks (the "shoulders"). When the stock breaks below the "neckline," it often indicates a downward trend.
- Double Top: A bearish reversal pattern where the stock hits the same high twice before falling. Think of it as the market saying, "That's as high as we're going."
- Double Bottom: The bullish counterpart to the Double Top. The stock hits the same low twice and then bounces upward, signaling a potential rally.
- Ascending Triangle: A bullish continuation pattern with a rising support line meeting a flat resistance line, suggesting a breakout upward.
- Descending Triangle: A bearish continuation pattern with a descending resistance line and a flat support line, often preceding a breakdown.
- Symmetrical Triangle: A neutral pattern where both support and resistance lines converge, indicating the

stock is coiling for a breakout—direction to be determined.

- <u>Flags and Pennants</u>: Short-term continuation patterns that look like small consolidations within a larger trend. They often signal that the stock will continue moving in the same direction.

Beyond patterns, technical analysis relies on tools like moving averages, which smooth out daily price fluctuations to highlight a stock's overall trend. The 50-day and 200-day moving averages are particularly popular, helping traders spot bullish "golden crosses" (when a short-term average crosses above a long-term average) or bearish "death crosses" (when the opposite happens).

Another popular tool is Fibonacci retracement levels, based on mathematical ratios derived from the Fibonacci sequence. These levels are used to identify potential support or resistance zones where the stock might reverse or consolidate. While some traders swear by Fibonacci's predictive power, others chalk it up to the market's tendency to reflect patterns wherever we choose to see them.

No technical analysis is complete without indicators—the high-tech gadgets of the trading world. The Relative Strength Index (RSI) measures whether a stock is overbought or oversold, while the Moving Average Convergence Divergence (MACD) helps traders spot changes in momentum. These tools offer extra layers of insight into price movements and can confirm—or contradict—the signals from chart patterns.

For short-term traders, technical analysis is like having a treasure map, albeit one with some ambiguous directions. It won't predict every market move with certainty, but it provides valuable clues for navigating the chaos. And whether you're decoding Head and Shoulders or watching for a golden cross, mastering these tools can make the market's mood swings a little less mysterious—and a lot more fun to analyze.

The Death Cross: A Bearish Signal in Action

The Death Cross—ominous in name, but not a harbinger of the apocalypse—is one of the most widely recognized bearish signals in technical analysis. It occurs when a stock's short-term moving average (usually the 50-day) crosses below its long-term moving average (typically the

200-day). Think of it as a breakup between short-term momentum and long-term optimism, with the chart announcing, "It's not me, it's you." This crossover suggests a potential long-term downtrend, making traders sit up and take notice—or possibly run for the exits.

One famous example of the Death Cross came in March 2020, during the early stages of the COVID-19 pandemic. As the world went into lockdown and uncertainty gripped the markets, the S&P 500 exhibited the dreaded crossover. The index's 50-day moving average dipped below the 200-day moving average, reflecting the sharp and sudden loss of investor confidence. Sure enough, the market continued to decline as fear peaked. However, this particular Death Cross came with a twist: thanks to unprecedented fiscal and monetary stimulus, the market rebounded in record time, turning a once-bearish signal into a mere blip on the long-term uptrend. It was as if the market said, "Just kidding!" and came roaring back.

How to Use the Death Cross

The Death Cross is like a red flag on the racetrack of trading—it signals caution, but it's not an absolute guarantee of disaster. When the short-term moving average falls below the long-term average, it suggests that downward momentum is gaining steam. Traders often use it to identify opportunities to sell, short a stock, or avoid entering a long position. But the real power of the Death Cross lies in pairing it with other indicators:

- **Volume Trends**: If the Death Cross is accompanied by a surge in trading volume, it strengthens the bearish signal, indicating that investors are collectively jumping ship.
- **RSI (Relative Strength Index)**: If the RSI also shows that a stock is overbought, the Death Cross becomes even more compelling. It's like the market saying, "Yep, we're tired, and it's time for a break."
- **Macro Context**: As seen in March 2020, external factors like economic conditions or central bank interventions can influence whether a Death Cross leads to a sustained downtrend or a quick recovery.

Limitations and Lessons

While the Death Cross has an intimidating name and often gets a lot of media attention, it's far from foolproof. Sometimes, it produces what traders call a "whipsaw," where the signal appears, traders act on it, and the stock or index promptly reverses direction. It's like getting all dressed up for a storm that turns into a drizzle. That's why it's best to use the Death Cross as one piece of the puzzle, rather than a standalone decision-making tool.

Despite its limitations, the Death Cross remains a valuable guidepost, especially when paired with other technical tools and a healthy dose of market context. It's a reminder that the market, much like life, is full of signals to interpret—but they're not always as scary as they sound. So the next time you hear about a Death Cross, don't panic. Just take a closer look, check the broader trends, and maybe crack a smile at the dramatic name for what is, at its heart, just another tool in a trader's toolbox.

Many More Technical Strategies

While the Death Cross grabs headlines with its dramatic name, it's just one of many tools in the technical analysis playbook. Golden Crosses signal the opposite—a bullish crossover where the 50-day moving average rises above the 200-day, often heralding upward momentum. Relative Strength Index (RSI) measures whether a stock is overbought or oversold, giving traders clues about potential reversals. Meanwhile, Fibonacci retracements use math (and a touch of market mysticism) to identify key levels of support and resistance. And then there's the MACD (Moving Average Convergence Divergence), a multitasker that tracks trend direction and momentum. Whether you're deciphering a Head and Shoulders pattern or following a Bollinger Band breakout, these signals all add color and context to the market's story, helping traders navigate the chaos with confidence.

Dividend Reinvestment Plans (DRIPs): Compounding Your Wealth

One of the simplest and most magical ways to grow your wealth in the stock market is through a **Dividend Reinvestment Plan**, affectionately known as a **DRIP.** Think of it as the gift that keeps on giving: instead of receiving your dividends as cash, a DRIP automatically reinvests them into more shares of the same stock. It's like planting a tree, watching it grow, and realizing it's not just bearing fruit—it's planting a whole orchard for you. Over time, the reinvested dividends start earning dividends of their own, creating a compounding snowball effect that can turn modest investments into impressive fortunes.

Imagine this: you own 50 shares of a company that pays a $1 annual dividend per share. Instead of pocketing that $50 and splurging on fancy coffee for a month, you reinvest it to buy more shares. Next year, you've got a little more stock and a little more dividend income. The cycle continues, and before long, your growing pile of shares starts generating dividends that make your original income look like pocket change. It's the ultimate financial self-perpetuating machine.

DRIPs are particularly appealing for a few reasons. First, they're a long-term investor's best friend. The longer you let those dividends compound, the more powerful the results. Second, they're perfect for small investors because many DRIPs let you buy fractional shares. That means even your smallest dividends are put to work—no loose change sitting idle here. And let's not forget the cost efficiency: most DRIPs come with no fees, which means more of your money stays invested where it belongs.

Over 20 years, a DRIP can transform a modest investment into a serious nest egg, especially if the underlying stock appreciates in value. It's the closest thing to "set it and forget it" that the stock market offers. So next time you're wondering what to do with those dividends, don't just spend them on lattes—let them do the heavy lifting and grow your financial forest instead.

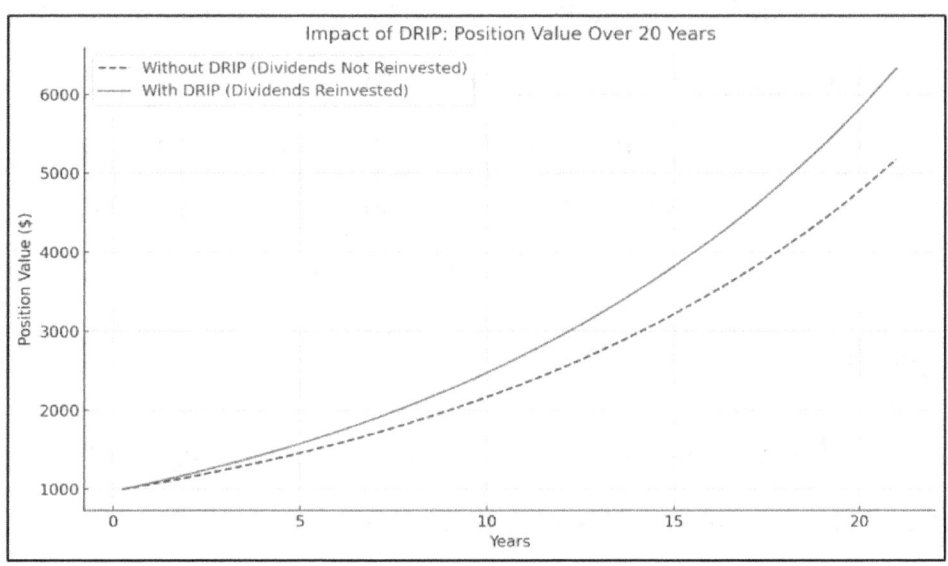

Figure 12: Value of Direct Reinvestment Plans

Day Trading: The Thrill and Agony of the Short Game

Day trading is the stock market's adrenaline junkie—fast-paced, high-stakes, and not for the faint of heart. Unlike the steady, methodical approach of long-term investing, day trading is all about quick decisions and short-term wins. Traders buy and sell stocks, options, or other assets within the same trading day, aiming to profit from small price movements. It's like a financial version of speed dating: quick, intense, and sometimes rewarding, but often leaving you wondering what just happened.

For those who master the art, day trading can be incredibly lucrative. But let's be honest—it's also an arena filled with risk, stress, and the ever-present possibility of seeing your hard-earned capital vanish faster than your New Year's resolutions. Successful day traders need sharp analytical skills, near-unbreakable discipline, and a healthy dose of capital to ride out the inevitable losing streaks.

The Nature of Day Trading

At its core, day trading revolves around exploiting volatility. Traders thrive on price fluctuations, scanning charts, studying technical indicators, and reacting to breaking news faster than a cheetah chasing lunch. Stocks, forex, and options are all fair game, provided they're liquid enough for rapid buying and selling. It's not uncommon for day traders to make dozens, even hundreds, of trades in a single day, each one a tiny chess move in a high-stakes game.

But make no mistake—this isn't some glamorous, "get rich quick" gig. Day trading requires hours of preparation, rigorous strategy testing, and the mental toughness to stick to a plan even when the market is trying to shake you off like a bucking bronco.

The Pattern Day Trading Rule

One of the first roadblocks many aspiring day traders encounter is the Pattern Day Trading (PDT) rule, a regulation designed to protect inexperienced traders from blowing up their accounts. According to the rule, if you execute four or more day trades within five business days using a margin account, you're flagged as a pattern day trader. To keep playing the game, you must maintain a minimum balance of $25,000 in your account. For beginners with smaller accounts, this rule is often a deal-breaker. It's the financial equivalent of a bouncer at an exclusive club saying, "You can come in, but only if you have this much cash in your pocket."

While some traders save up to meet the requirement, others look for ways to bypass it, such as trading in cash accounts or exploring prop trading firms, which we'll get to in a moment. However, the PDT rule serves as a reality check: day trading is capital-intensive, and the barrier to entry is high for a reason.

High Risk, High Stress

If the thought of rollercoaster volatility and watching your portfolio swing wildly in minutes gives you anxiety, day trading might not be for you. The high-risk nature of the business means losses can pile up quickly, especially for those without a solid risk management plan. One bad trade—or a string of them—can wipe out weeks or months of progress. Day traders live by the mantra, "Cut your losses quickly," but sticking to that advice in the heat of the moment is easier said than done.

The stress of day trading isn't just financial—it's also psychological. The pressure to make split-second decisions while staring at blinking screens and ever-changing numbers is enough to test anyone's nerves. Add in the fear of missing out (FOMO) on a big move or the pain of taking an early loss only to see the stock bounce back, and you've got a recipe for serious mental strain. Many traders joke that day trading is like a video game, except the "game over" screen comes with real financial consequences.

Trading for a Prop Firm

For those who have the skills but not the cash to meet the PDT rule, proprietary trading firms, or prop firms, offer a unique opportunity. Prop firms let traders use the company's capital to trade in exchange for a cut of the profits. In some cases, traders must put up a small amount of their own money as a risk deposit, but the leverage provided by the firm allows for much larger trades than an individual could afford on their own.

Think of it as a trading apprenticeship: the firm provides tools, training, and capital, and you provide the strategy and execution. Firms like Topstep, FTMO, and others cater to aspiring traders willing to prove their mettle. However, these opportunities come with conditions. Prop firms have strict rules on risk management, and failure to comply can mean losing access to the account. While it's a great way to gain experience and scale up, trading with someone else's money can add a new layer of stress—there's nothing like knowing a firm is watching your every move to keep you on your toes.

Is Day Trading for You?

Day trading is exhilarating, challenging, and potentially rewarding, but it's not for everyone. It demands time, dedication, and the ability to weather financial and emotional ups and downs. It's a high-stakes game where the potential for big wins is matched only by the risk of devastating losses. For those who thrive on adrenaline, have a disciplined approach, and love the thrill of the markets, it can be the ultimate test of trading skill. For everyone else, it's a reminder that sometimes slow and steady really does win the race.

Whether you're a seasoned trader or a curious observer, one thing is certain: day trading is a world of its own, filled with big risks, bigger egos, and the occasional victory dance when everything goes right. Just don't forget to breathe—it's a marathon, not a sprint. Well, sort of.

A Cautionary Tale

There is a widely cited statistic that over 90% of day traders lose money, and it's often used to caution aspiring traders about the harsh realities of the business. While the exact figure varies depending on the source, multiple studies have confirmed that the majority of individual day traders fail to turn a profit consistently.

For example, a 2019 study from Brazil examined over 1,500 day traders over a period of five years. The findings? Only 3% made any profit at all, and less than 1% earned enough to be considered a meaningful income. Another study from Taiwan in 2004 found that less than 20% of day traders were profitable, and even among those, only a small fraction consistently outperformed the market.

The reasons for this high failure rate are manifold:

1. **Lack of Skill and Knowledge**: Many new traders jump in without understanding the complexities of the market, mistaking fast trades for easy money.
2. **High Costs**: Frequent trading incurs transaction fees and taxes, which can eat into profits faster than most realize.
3. **Emotional Decisions**: Day trading is a psychological game, and fear, greed, or FOMO (fear of missing out) often lead to poor decision-making.
4. **Competition with Professionals**: Individual traders are often up against institutional investors, algorithms, and high-frequency traders who have more resources, faster execution speeds, and greater expertise.

This doesn't mean that profitable day trading is impossible, but the odds are undeniably steep. The statistic serves as a reality check: the stock market isn't an ATM, and the road to consistent profitability is paved with education, discipline, and often, losses. For most, the safer (and saner) bet is sticking to long-term investing strategies.

A Day in the Life of Jake, the Day Trader

Jake's alarm blares at 5:30 a.m., but he's already awake. Sleep isn't exactly easy when you know the market could make—or break—you today. He brews a strong pot of coffee, grabs his phone, and dives into the morning's headlines: "Tech Giant Beats Earnings Expectations" catches his eye. Perfect—volatility is his playground, and this stock might be his star player today.

By 6:00 a.m., Jake is in his home office, surrounded by three monitors flashing charts, news feeds, and his trading platform. He reviews his watchlist, focusing on stocks showing pre-market volume spikes. A biotech stock that's up 15% on promising trial results makes the cut, along with a semiconductor company riding on a bullish upgrade. He scribbles his game plan in his notebook: buy breakout above $200, sell target at $210, stop-loss at $195.

The market opens at 9:30 a.m., and Jake's adrenaline spikes. His first trade is a classic breakout play. The semiconductor stock surges past $200, and he pulls the trigger, buying 500 shares. The price moves up quickly, hitting $203 within minutes, but Jake notices a sudden dip in volume—a red flag. He exits at $202.50, pocketing $1,250. "Not bad for 15 minutes," he mutters, taking a quick sip of coffee, now lukewarm.

But not every trade goes so smoothly. Around 10:15 a.m., Jake spots a biotech stock forming a triangle pattern. He buys in at $45, expecting a breakout, but the stock reverses. Before he can react, it plummets to $43. Jake slams his desk in frustration, taking a $1,000 loss. "Stick to your stops, Jake," he mutters, shaking his head.

By lunchtime, the action slows. Jake uses the midday lull to review his morning trades. The wins feel good, but the loss stings. He reminds himself that discipline is key. His phone buzzes with a text from a friend: "How's the market treating you?" Jake replies with a smirking emoji and "Same old battlefield."

The afternoon brings another opportunity—a retail stock breaking out on news of record holiday sales. Jake jumps in at $120, aiming for a quick scalp. The stock inches higher, hitting $121. Jake considers holding for more, but he remembers his earlier mistake and exits for a modest $500 gain. "Greed kills," he reminds himself.

The market closes at 4:00 p.m., but Jake's day isn't over. He spends an hour reviewing his trades in detail, logging them in his journal. His P&L (profit and loss) for the day shows $750—up overall, but a far cry from the big wins he dreamed of this morning. He adjusts his watchlist for tomorrow, focusing on stocks with upcoming earnings reports and tight technical setups.

As Jake finally steps away from his desk, he feels both drained and exhilarated. Day trading is a grind—one that tests his patience, discipline, and ego every single day. Some days are spectacular, others humbling. But for Jake, it's not just a job. It's a challenge, a puzzle, and, yes, a thrill ride he can't resist.

Stock Options: The Art and Science of Leverage

Stock options are like the power tools of the investing world—capable of amazing results when used correctly but also capable of disaster in the wrong hands. They provide a way to amplify your potential gains with much less capital than buying stocks outright, but that same leverage can magnify losses if things go sideways. At their core, options are contracts that give you the right—but not the obligation—to buy (call options) or sell (put options) a stock at a specific price before a set expiration date. This flexibility, combined with their versatility, makes options a favorite tool for everyone from cautious income investors to thrill-seeking speculators.

Option Basics: The Building Blocks of a Trade

Before diving into strategies, it's essential to understand the language and mechanics of options. Think of this as learning the rules of the road before driving a Ferrari.

An option contract represents 100 shares of the underlying stock, meaning a single contract gives you control over a lot more shares than you could afford outright. The strike price is the agreed-upon price at which the stock can be bought (in the case of a call) or sold (in the case of a put). The expiration date marks the deadline for making your move—after that, the option expires worthless if it's not exercised or sold.

Options come in various flavors depending on their timeframes. Monthly options are the most common and expire on the third Friday of each month. For more active traders, weekly options provide shorter-term opportunities, expiring every Friday. And for those with nerves of steel, daily options—available on some indices—let you trade with razor-thin margins of time.

Not all stocks have options available. The underlying stocks must meet specific criteria, including liquidity and price stability, to be optionable. And options themselves are priced using premiums, determined by factors like the stock's price, volatility, and time remaining until expiration.

Now that you know the basics, let's talk strategy.

Put Selling: Getting Paid to Wait

Put selling is a conservative way to use options, perfect for investors who want to buy stocks at a discount. When you sell a put, you agree to buy a stock at a specific price if it drops to that level, and in return, you collect a premium upfront. If the stock doesn't fall, you keep the premium as pure profit. If it does, you buy the stock at the agreed price—often lower than the market price, thanks to the premium you received.

For instance, if you're eyeing a stock trading at $50 but think it's a better deal at $45, you could sell a $45 put for $2. If the stock stays above $45, you pocket the $200 premium (for one contract) without lifting a finger. If it drops, you end up owning the stock at an effective cost of $43 per share ($45 strike price minus the $2 premium). It's a win-win strategy, provided the stock doesn't completely tank.

Covered Call Selling: Renting Out Your Stocks

If you already own a stock and want to generate extra income, selling covered calls might be your best bet. By selling a call option, you agree to sell your shares at a specific price if the stock rises above that level. In return, you collect a premium. If the stock doesn't hit the strike price, you keep your shares and the premium. If it does, you sell your shares at the strike price, still keeping the premium as a bonus.

For example, suppose you own 100 shares of a stock trading at $100. You sell a call with a strike price of $105 for $2. If the stock stays below $105, you keep your shares and the $200 premium. If it rises above $105, your shares get sold, but you effectively earn $107 per share ($105 strike price plus the $2 premium). It's a great way to earn "rental income" from your stocks while potentially cashing out at a higher price.

Speculative Trades: Swinging for the Fences

For traders looking for big wins with limited capital, speculative options trades are the name of the game. Instead of buying a stock outright, you purchase options that give you exposure to potential price movements at a fraction of the cost.

Imagine Stock XYZ is trading at $50, and you think it's heading to $60 within a month. Instead of spending $5,000 to buy 100 shares, you buy a call option with a $50 strike price for $200. If the stock hits $60, your option could be worth $1,000—a 400% gain. But if the stock doesn't move or drops below $50, your option expires worthless, and you're out $200. It's high risk, high reward, and not for the faint of heart.

Stock Replacement: Leveraging Smarter

Stock replacement is a savvy way to use options to mimic stock ownership while tying up less capital. By buying deep-in-the-money call options, you get the upside potential of the stock without having to purchase it outright.

Suppose Stock ABC is trading at $100. Instead of buying 100 shares for $10,000, you buy a call option with a $70 strike price for $35 (or $3,500 for 100 shares worth of control). If the stock rises to $120, your option gains nearly as much as the stock would have, but you've risked far less capital. It's an excellent strategy for those who want to leverage their portfolio without going all-in.

The Balancing Act: Risks and Rewards

Options are powerful tools, but they require a deep understanding of the market and a clear strategy. The leverage they offer can amplify returns while limiting risk to the premium paid. However, their time-sensitive nature means they can expire worthless if your bet doesn't pay off.

Whether you're selling puts for income, writing covered calls on your existing stocks, or using options to speculate on price movements, the key is discipline and planning. Options can be a game-changer for savvy investors, offering flexibility, income potential, and risk management tools that traditional stock ownership simply can't match. Just remember: with great leverage comes great responsibility—and maybe a little heartburn during volatile trading sessions.

ETFs: The One-Stop Shop for Modern Investing

Exchange-Traded Funds, or ETFs, are the stock market's version of the buffet: a little bit of everything on your plate, without the hassle of choosing each dish. An ETF is a basket of securities—stocks, bonds, commodities, or a mix—that trades on an exchange like an individual stock. With just one purchase, you can invest in an entire index, sector, or strategy. It's a simplified, efficient, and cost-effective way to build a diversified portfolio, making ETFs a favorite tool for both beginners and seasoned pros.

A Brief History of ETFs: From SPY to "Wait, What Does This ETF Do?"

The ETF revolution began in 1993 with the launch of the SPDR S&P 500 ETF (SPY), designed to track the performance of the S&P 500 index. SPY was the first widely traded ETF, giving investors exposure to 500 of the largest U.S. companies in a single trade. It was a game-changer, allowing everyday investors to buy into the entire market without needing to own all 500 stocks individually.

Not long after, the Invesco QQQ Trust (QQQ) hit the scene in 1999, offering exposure to the tech-heavy Nasdaq-100. This ETF quickly became a go-to for investors wanting to ride the wave of innovation, capturing stocks like Apple, Microsoft, and Amazon. If SPY was the sensible sedan of ETFs, QQQ was the shiny sports car, delivering higher volatility and potentially bigger returns.

From these humble beginnings, the ETF universe exploded. Today, there are thousands of ETFs covering every imaginable corner of the market. Want exposure to clean energy stocks? There's an ETF for that. Interested in dividend-paying companies? Covered. How about high-yield bonds, commodities like gold, or even themes like the metaverse or artificial intelligence? Yep, there's an ETF for that too. ETFs have gone from a few broad-market options to a full-blown carnival of choices, catering to every niche interest and investment strategy.

Why ETFs Are So Popular: The Perks of Passive Investing
Diversification Made Simple

One of the biggest selling points of ETFs is instant diversification. When you buy an ETF, you're not putting all your eggs in one basket; you're buying into a basket of eggs from many baskets. A single S&P 500 ETF like SPY gives you exposure to 500 different companies across various industries, significantly reducing the risk of any one company's failure dragging down your portfolio.

Low Costs That Won't Break the Bank

ETFs are notorious for their low expense ratios, which are the annual fees you pay to the fund managers. Many broad-market ETFs charge less than 0.1% per year—that's just $1 on a $1,000 investment. Compare that to the 1% or more charged by many mutual funds, and you see why ETFs are a cost-conscious investor's dream.

Liquidity You Can Count On

Unlike mutual funds, which only trade once per day after the market closes, ETFs trade like stocks. You can buy or sell them at any time during market hours. Whether you're seizing an opportunity or making a quick exit, ETFs offer the flexibility to act immediately.

Tax Efficiency

ETFs are also more tax-efficient than traditional mutual funds. Because of how they're structured, ETFs rarely distribute capital gains to investors, meaning you won't owe taxes unless you sell your shares. It's like having your cake and not paying taxes on it—well, until you take a bite.

The Many Flavors of ETFs: Pick Your Investment Adventure

Today's ETF market is like a giant Baskin-Robbins with more flavors than you knew existed. Here are just a few of the categories you'll encounter:

- Broad Market ETFs: These are the classics, like SPY, QQQ, or Vanguard's Total Stock Market ETF (VTI), which offer exposure to the entire market or major indices. They're the financial equivalent of vanilla—reliable, consistent, and always in style.

- Sector ETFs: Want to bet on a specific part of the market, like technology, healthcare, or renewable energy? Sector ETFs let you zoom in on industries you believe in. The ARK Innovation ETF (ARKK), for example, targets cutting-edge tech companies and has become a favorite for investors seeking high-growth opportunities.

- Dividend ETFs: These funds focus on stocks that pay consistent dividends, making them popular among income-focused investors. Examples include the Vanguard High Dividend Yield ETF (VYM) or the Schwab U.S. Dividend Equity ETF (SCHD).

- Thematic ETFs: Feeling adventurous? Thematic ETFs target niche areas like esports, cannabis, or even space exploration. While they're fun and trendy, be careful—these funds often carry higher risk and volatility.

- High-Yield ETFs: For investors seeking income, there are ETFs focused on high-yield bonds, REITs (Real Estate Investment Trusts), or preferred stocks. These can provide steady cash flow, but with higher yields often comes higher risk.

Leveraging ETFs: Strategies for Every Investor

ETFs aren't just for passive buy-and-hold investors; they can also be used in more active strategies. For instance, sector ETFs allow traders to make targeted bets on which parts of the market will outperform. Meanwhile, bond ETFs can help stabilize a portfolio, and leveraged ETFs (which aim to double or triple the daily performance of an index) let risk-tolerant traders amplify their returns—or losses.

For example, if you believe the tech sector is poised for a rebound, buying a tech-focused ETF like QQQ or XLK lets you capitalize on that thesis without picking individual stocks. On the flip side, if you're concerned about market volatility, ETFs like VIXY (tracking volatility) or bond-focused funds like BND can provide a hedge.

The Risks of ETFs: Not All That Glitters Is Gold

Despite their many advantages, ETFs aren't without risks. Niche and thematic ETFs, in particular, can be highly volatile and heavily concentrated in specific stocks or sectors. Leveraged ETFs, while tempting for their promise of outsized returns, can magnify losses just as quickly. It's also worth noting that not all ETFs are created equal—expense ratios, tracking error, and liquidity vary widely. Always read the fine print before diving in.

Why ETFs Are Here to Stay

Since their debut, ETFs have revolutionized the investing world by democratizing access to the market. They're easy to use, cost-effective, and versatile, offering solutions for virtually every investment goal. Whether you're a beginner looking to dip your toes into the market or a seasoned pro fine-tuning your strategy, ETFs provide a tool that's as simple or sophisticated as you need it to be.

And let's face it—who doesn't want a diversified portfolio without the hassle of analyzing individual stocks? ETFs are the ultimate investing shortcut, letting you ride the market's waves without feeling like you're drowning in research. So go ahead, grab an ETF, and let your portfolio work smarter, not harder.

Risk Assessment: Balancing Reward and Risk

The stock market offers a spectrum of risk levels:

- **Long-Term Investing (2 to 3)**: Diversified portfolios of index funds or dividend stocks carry lower risks and steady returns.
- **Day Trading (4 to 5)**: High volatility and rapid decisions make day trading one of the riskiest strategies.
- **Options Speculation (4 to 5)**: Options carry high potential rewards but require skill to avoid significant losses.

Final Thoughts

The stock market offers a wealth of opportunities for every type of investor, from those seeking long-term growth to thrill-seekers chasing short-term gains. By understanding tools like DRIPs, ETFs, and technical and fundamental analysis, you can craft a strategy tailored to your goals and risk tolerance. With patience and discipline, the stock market can help you turn $100 into a foundation for financial success.

Collectibles – Investing in Nostalgia and Scarcity

Collectibles occupy a unique space in the investment world, blending the thrill of ownership with the potential for financial reward. From rare coins and vintage art to baseball cards and designer sneakers, the value of collectibles is driven by cultural trends, nostalgia, and scarcity. Unlike stocks or bonds, these items are tangible, often carrying personal meaning or historical significance. For many, investing in collectibles is as much about passion as it is about profit.

But investing in collectibles isn't a one-way street to wealth. The market ebbs and flows, influenced by generational shifts and emotional connections. Nostalgia—a powerful driver of value—often peaks when a particular generation reaches its prime earning years. At the same time, markets can wane as those same collectors age out or lose interest, causing prices to fall. Understanding these dynamics is key to navigating the collectibles market wisely.

Why Collectibles Hold Value

The value of collectibles comes from a mix of emotional and financial factors. Scarcity, cultural relevance, and condition play critical roles, but at its heart, the market is fueled by desire. Collectibles tap into something personal: a connection to youth, a piece of history, or a symbol of status. For example, a rare first-edition comic book or a pristine set of baseball cards can evoke deep nostalgia for a particular time and place.

Consider this: in the 1980s and 1990s, baby boomers poured money into antique furniture, fine china, and vintage cars, driving prices sky-high. These items reminded them of their parents' homes and their own childhoods. Today, millennials and Gen Z are driving entirely different markets—vintage sneakers, Pokémon cards, retro video games, and even NFTs—items that reflect their own upbringing in the digital and pop culture eras.

This cycle of nostalgia and financial capacity creates windows of opportunity. Prices soar when a generation hits its peak earning years, only to fade as interest wanes or another generation's preferences take center stage. For investors, timing and cultural awareness are critical.

The Generational Flow of Value

Nostalgia is a fickle force. A collectible that is highly sought after today could see its value decline dramatically a few decades later. The rise and fall of interest in specific categories often follows the life cycle of a generation. For example, collectors of vintage baseball cards in the 1980s were largely baby boomers rediscovering their childhood passions. As their disposable income grew, so did demand for cards featuring legends like Mickey Mantle or Babe Ruth.

Fast forward to today, and many of those same collectors are in their twilight years. Some are selling their collections, flooding the market with supply, while younger generations show less interest in traditional sports memorabilia. This generational shift has caused the values of many mid-century collectibles to plateau—or even decline.

On the flip side, consider Pokémon cards. Millennials and Gen Z, who grew up during Pokémon's heyday, now have disposable income and are driving prices to astronomical levels. A first-edition Charizard card recently sold for over $400,000, fueled by nostalgia and scarcity. But as this generation ages and their interests evolve, the market may eventually cool, leaving those who bought at peak prices with diminished returns.

Examples of Popular Collectibles

Collectibles come in many forms, from timeless classics to modern trends. Let's explore a few categories and what makes them appealing.

1. Rare Coins and Precious Metals

Coins are among the most enduring collectibles, valued for both their historical significance and intrinsic metal content. A rare gold coin like the Saint-Gaudens Double Eagle combines scarcity, craftsmanship, and a connection to history. Coins tend to hold value well, as they appeal to both collectors and investors seeking a hedge against inflation.

2. Trading Cards

The trading card market has experienced a massive resurgence. Sports cards featuring legends like Michael Jordan or rookie cards of contemporary stars like Patrick Mahomes are in high demand. Similarly, gaming cards like Pokémon and Magic: The Gathering have become cultural icons, blending nostalgia with fierce competition among collectors.

3. Art and Antiques

Fine art has long been a playground for wealthy investors, but fractional ownership platforms like Masterworks have made it accessible to smaller investors. Antiques, from vintage furniture to historical artifacts, also hold value, though trends in this market can be cyclical. For example, mid-century modern furniture has surged in popularity, while ornate Victorian pieces have fallen out of favor.

4. Sneakers and Streetwear

The sneaker market has become a multi-billion-dollar industry. Limited-edition releases from brands like Nike and Adidas are often resold for many times their retail price. Sneakers combine scarcity with status, particularly among younger generations. For instance, Kanye West's Nike Air Yeezy prototypes sold for $1.8 million, demonstrating the cultural clout of this market.

5. Pop Culture Memorabilia

Items like original Star Wars action figures, signed movie posters, or vintage video game consoles are booming in value. These items tap directly into the nostalgia of millennials and Gen Z, who are willing to pay a premium for pieces of their childhood.

6. Comic Books

From Superman's debut in Action Comics #1 to Marvel's early issues, comic books are cultural artifacts as well as financial assets. As superhero franchises dominate Hollywood, interest in original comic books has surged, driving prices higher.

7. Emerging Categories

Modern collectibles like NFTs (non-fungible tokens) are pushing the boundaries of what constitutes a collectible. Digital art, music, and even virtual real estate are gaining traction, though they carry significant risk due to their novelty and volatility.

What to Consider Before Investing

Investing in collectibles is as much an art as it is a science. To succeed, you need to develop expertise in your chosen category and approach each purchase with care.

1. **Condition**: Items in mint condition fetch the highest prices. Even slight damage can significantly reduce value. Professional grading services can authenticate and assess collectibles, ensuring you're paying a fair price.
2. **Authenticity**: Fraud is rampant in the collectibles world. Always buy from reputable dealers or use third-party verification services.
3. **Scarcity**: The rarer the item, the higher its value—at least in theory. However, scarcity alone isn't enough; demand must also be present.
4. **Cultural Trends**: Timing matters. Understanding which generation is driving demand can help you decide when to buy or sell.
5. **Storage and Maintenance**: Collectibles require proper care to retain value. Coins should be stored in protective cases, art needs climate control, and sneakers must be kept in pristine condition.

Value is in the Eye of the Bidder

Determining the value of collectibles is as much an art as it is a science. While there are professional appraisers, price guides, and online marketplaces offering ballpark figures, the truth is that value is often in the eye of the beholder—or, more accurately, the wallet of the buyer. Two experts might look at the same item and come up with wildly different estimates, influenced by factors like rarity, condition, market trends, and even personal nostalgia. A Mickey Mantle card might be priceless to one baseball fan but "just a piece of cardboard" to someone else. Ultimately, the real value of any collectible boils down to what someone is willing to pay for it at that moment in time. The auction room, with its heated bidding wars, often provides the truest test of worth. As the saying goes, "An item's value isn't set by what it's listed for—it's set by the highest bidder who refuses to back down." So, while guides and appraisals are helpful, they're only part of the equation. The magic happens when the right item meets the right buyer at just the right time.

Top Resources for Collectible Appraisal

Determining the value of collectibles can be a tricky endeavor, but there are plenty of resources to guide collectors. Online marketplaces like eBay, Heritage Auctions, and Sotheby's often provide a snapshot of current market trends through auction results and active listings. For more specialized insights, platforms like Beckett (for trading cards), PSA (Professional Sports Authenticator), and NonFungible.com (for NFTs) offer tools and services to appraise or track collectible values. Local collectibles shops and appraisers can also be invaluable, providing in-person expertise and authenticity checks. Additionally, forums and collector communities, such as Reddit threads or Facebook groups, can be great for peer insights, though opinions may vary widely. Ultimately, no resource is perfect, so cross-referencing multiple sources and staying updated on market trends is key to pinpointing value.

Case Study: The Unexpected Fortune of "Grandpa's Junk Drawer"

When Sarah inherited her grandfather's house, she wasn't exactly thrilled about the task of cleaning it out. The attic was packed with everything from dusty old books to tin cans full of screws—and then there was "The Junk Drawer." It was the sort of drawer that defied physics, stuffed with everything from mismatched buttons to what looked like a petrified sandwich. Hidden among the chaos, Sarah discovered a small box of baseball cards wrapped in a rubber band that crumbled to dust at her touch.

She almost tossed the cards into the trash but paused. "Wait," she thought. "People collect these things, right?" She snapped a picture of the cards and posted it in a local collectibles forum with the caption: *"Found these in my grandpa's junk. Any of them worth keeping, or should I use them as bookmarks?"*

Within minutes, her inbox blew up. "Is that a 1952 Topps Mickey Mantle?!" one user typed in all caps, followed by several emojis and what appeared to be the outline of a fainting person. Another person offered her $5,000 on the spot, "just to save you the hassle of looking up prices."

Skeptical but curious, Sarah decided to dig deeper. She Googled the card and discovered it was one of the most sought-after collectibles in the world. "Mickey Mantle, huh?" she muttered. "Never heard of him, but okay."

The Appraisal: A Wild Ride

Sarah took the cards to a professional appraiser. The man practically drooled as he flipped through the deck. "These are in incredible condition," he said, squinting at her over his glasses. He explained that while the Mantle card was the crown jewel, the collection also included several rare rookie cards that could fetch thousands of dollars each.

Sarah's mind boggled. She had been about to throw them out, and now this dusty little box was worth more than her car. "Are you sure this isn't some kind of prank?" she asked. The appraiser chuckled and assured her it was very real.

The Auction: From Junk to Jackpot

Sarah decided to auction the collection through a reputable auction house. The bidding war for the Mickey Mantle card alone was intense, climbing higher and higher until it finally sold for $2.1 million. That's right—million. As Sarah watched the final bid roll in, she couldn't help but laugh. "Grandpa's junk drawer just paid off my mortgage," she joked to the auctioneer.

The Lessons Learned

1. Don't Judge a Drawer by Its Dust: That box of "junk" turned out to be a gold mine. When in doubt, do a little research before tossing things out.
2. Authenticity Matters: Sarah's cards were so valuable because they were genuine and in excellent condition. If she had tried to clean or handle them carelessly, she could have accidentally reduced their value.
3. Sometimes Luck Beats Strategy: Sarah didn't set out to become a collector; she just got lucky. But her decision to check before trashing turned her fortune around.

As Sarah put it in a social media post later: *"Thanks, Grandpa. I'll never look at a junk drawer the same way again."*

NFTs: Collectibles for the Digital Frontier

Let's face it—NFTs are the new kid on the collectible block, and they're not here to play by the old rules. Unlike physical collectibles that you can hold, display, or accidentally spill coffee on, NFTs exist entirely in the digital realm. Imagine buying a piece of art that you can't hang on your wall but can proudly showcase on your phone or as a profile picture on social media. Welcome to the future of bragging rights.

At their core, NFTs are about ownership. Powered by blockchain technology, they provide proof that you own something unique in the digital universe, whether it's a piece of pixelated art, a meme-worthy GIF, or even a plot of virtual land in a metaverse you'll probably never set foot in. But let's be honest—it takes a leap of imagination to get excited about owning something you can't physically touch. It's like buying a star and naming it after your dog: meaningful to you, but a head-scratcher to others.

Supply, Demand, and a Sprinkle of Chaos

Here's where it gets interesting. The laws of supply and demand seem to apply to NFTs—kind of. Some NFTs are minted as part of a limited series, creating artificial scarcity that drives up their value. But then there are creators who mint hundreds or even thousands of similar assets, flooding the market with so many digital apes, cats, and aliens that you start to wonder if they're trying to recreate Noah's Ark on the blockchain.

The limitless potential supply of digital assets can muddy the waters for collectors trying to gauge value. After all, unlike a rare coin or a vintage baseball card, you can't run out of pixels. Still, scarcity isn't the only driver. Much like traditional art, the value of an NFT often hinges on hype, community engagement, and the inexplicable whims of internet culture. If you've ever seen a million-dollar GIF of a rainbow-puking cat, you know exactly what I mean.

A Generational Shift

While skeptics might scoff at the idea of paying thousands—or millions—for a digital image, there's no denying that NFTs are resonating with the digital-native generation. For many millennials and Gen Zers, the idea of owning a digital collectible feels as natural as buying a pair of designer sneakers to flex on Instagram. As this generation grows into its financial prime, it's likely we'll see NFTs become even more entrenched in the collectibles market.

But let's not pretend this is a smooth ride. Price volatility is the name of the game here. One day, your NFT of a pixelated punk might be worth enough to buy a Tesla; the next, it might be worth about as much as the latte you spilled on your non-digital collectibles. If there's a rule of thumb for NFT investing, it's this: only spend what you can afford to lose, and maybe double-check that you're actually buying the *right* NFT. (Remember the guy who thought he bought a Banksy NFT but ended up with an unrelated JPEG? Yikes.)

Will Digital Assets Have Their Day in the Sun?

It's too early to say if NFTs are a passing trend or the foundation of a new era in collecting, but one thing is clear: they're not going away anytime soon. As more industries adopt blockchain technology and more people embrace the digital age, the appeal of owning unique, authenticated digital assets will likely grow. Who knows? In a few decades, we might laugh at the idea of anyone doubting NFTs, much like people used to scoff at buying art prints or limited-edition sneakers.

Until then, NFT collecting is like the Wild West: full of opportunity, excitement, and just a little bit of chaos. Whether you're in it for the art, the investment potential, or the sheer novelty, it's a brave new world out there. Just make sure your digital wallet is as ready as your sense of humor.

NFTs 101: Where to Buy, Create, and Store Your Digital Assets

NFTs can be purchased, created, and stored using various online platforms and tools. Major marketplaces like OpenSea, Rarible, and Magic Eden are popular for buying and selling NFTs, while platforms like Foundation and SuperRare cater to exclusive, high-end collections. If you're feeling creative, you can mint your own NFTs on platforms like OpenSea or specialized tools like Mintable, where you upload your digital assets and set the terms. Once you've bought or minted your NFTs, you'll need a digital wallet—such as MetaMask, Coinbase Wallet, or Trust Wallet—to securely store and manage them. Just make sure to double-check wallet compatibility with your chosen platform and always safeguard your private keys to avoid digital heartbreak.

Risk Assessment: The Perils of Collectibles

On our **Risk Scale**, collectibles generally fall between **3 and 5**, depending on the category:

- **Coins and Precious Metals (3)**: These tend to hold value due to their intrinsic worth.

- **Trading Cards, Sneakers, and Pop Culture Memorabilia (4 to 5)**: These markets can be highly volatile, influenced by trends and generational preferences.
- **NFTs (4 to 5)**: These markets are just now emerging and too new to know what will be valuable and what will be lost in the hard drive of your old computer or a dusty corner of the cloud.

While collectibles can deliver extraordinary returns, they are often illiquid and subject to rapid changes in value. While over time these can be winners, often it just requires the time to pass. So, the best strategy here is likely to go ahead and put it in the safe or that dusty footlocker and check in every couple years.

Final Thoughts

Collectibles are a fascinating intersection of passion and profit. They are real assets and can allow you to turn hobbies and nostalgia into financial opportunities, but financial success requires knowledge, timing, and care. Whether you're drawn to vintage coins, trading cards, or modern sneakers, understanding the generational ebb and flow of demand is key. After all, the market for yesterday's treasures depends on today's buyers—and their memories of the past.

Cryptocurrency – Digital Gold or Fool's Gold?

Cryptocurrency has taken the financial world by storm over the past decade. Once dismissed as a fringe experiment, digital currencies like Bitcoin and Ethereum have emerged as mainstream assets, attracting everyone from tech-savvy millennials to institutional investors. With the promise of decentralization, transparency, and outsized returns, cryptocurrencies have been hailed as the future of money. But they've also been criticized for their volatility, regulatory uncertainty, and lack of intrinsic value. So, where does crypto fit in as an investment?

This chapter dives into the fascinating world of cryptocurrency, exploring how it works, why it's so polarizing, and whether it deserves a spot in your portfolio.

What Is Cryptocurrency?

At its core, cryptocurrency is digital money built on blockchain technology, a decentralized ledger that records transactions across a network of computers. Unlike traditional currencies issued by governments (fiat money), cryptocurrencies are not controlled by any central authority. This decentralized nature makes crypto appealing to those who value privacy, independence, and the potential for global transactions without intermediaries.

Bitcoin, created in 2009, was the first cryptocurrency and remains the most well-known. Its original purpose was to serve as a peer-to-peer payment system, but it has since evolved into a "store of value," often referred to as "digital gold." Ethereum, on the other hand, goes beyond payments, offering a platform for building decentralized applications (dApps) and smart contracts. Beyond these two giants, there are thousands of cryptocurrencies, each with its unique use case, market niche, and level of risk.

Blockchain: Reinventing Trust in a Digital World

Blockchain is the engine that powers cryptocurrency, but its transformative potential goes far beyond digital coins. At its core, blockchain is a decentralized, tamper-proof ledger that records transactions across a network of computers. Unlike traditional systems controlled by a central authority, blockchain operates on transparency and consensus, making it nearly impossible to alter or hack. This revolutionary technology enables trust in environments where trust doesn't naturally exist—whether it's verifying supply chains, automating contracts with precision, or enabling secure international payments in seconds. Blockchain is transformative because it removes middlemen, reduces costs, and dramatically increases efficiency across industries like finance, healthcare, logistics, and beyond. In short, it's not just reinventing the wheel—it's reinventing the entire road.

ow Blockchain Works: A Transparent Ledger in Action

Imagine you and your friends decide to track who owes money for group dinners, but instead of relying on one person to keep a written record (who may "accidentally" forget their own tab), everyone gets a copy of the ledger.

Now, every time someone pays or owes, all the ledgers update simultaneously. This is the essence of blockchain: a shared, decentralized ledger where every transaction is recorded, verified, and permanently stored.

Here's how it works: When a transaction is initiated—let's say you're transferring Bitcoin to a friend—it's grouped with other transactions into a "block." This block is then broadcast to a network of computers, or nodes, that validate the transactions through complex algorithms. Once verified, the block is added to a chain of previous blocks, creating a secure and chronological record. Importantly, every block contains a unique digital fingerprint (a hash) that ties it to the block before it, making tampering almost impossible. If anyone tries to alter a past transaction, the entire chain would break, and the network would reject it.

For a real-world analogy, think about buying a house. In traditional systems, you'd rely on lawyers, banks, and title companies to verify ownership and complete the transaction. With blockchain, the process is automated and transparent: the ownership record exists securely on the blockchain, and once your payment is validated, the ownership transfers to you instantly, with all parties able to see and confirm the transaction. No middlemen, no delays—just pure efficiency. That's the magic of blockchain: it combines trust, transparency, and security into a single, elegant system.

The Case for Investing in Cryptocurrency

If you've ever wanted to feel like a rebel investor while secretly hoping to become the next crypto millionaire, cryptocurrency might be calling your name. It's not just a speculative play anymore—though let's be honest, it's got all the rollercoaster thrills of a Vegas slot machine. Cryptocurrencies like Bitcoin and Ethereum have cemented themselves as more than just digital Monopoly money; they're quickly becoming a legitimate asset class with real-world use cases, scarcity, and the potential to disrupt entire industries. Let's explore why dipping your toes into the crypto waters might just be the bold move your portfolio needs.

Scarcity: The Digital Gold Rush

Imagine a vault with a finite number of treasures locked inside, and the key to opening it is getting harder to find every day. That's Bitcoin in a nutshell. With only 21 million coins ever to be mined, it's like the rarest collectible ever—

except instead of gathering dust on a shelf, it's a constantly evolving, decentralized powerhouse.

This supply limitation creates the kind of scarcity that drives value over time. It's the same principle that keeps gold prices high—except Bitcoin is far easier to transport. (Good luck stuffing a gold bar into your digital wallet.) As more investors, companies, and even entire countries hop on the Bitcoin bandwagon, the demand is climbing while the supply stays fixed. Economics 101 tells us that's a recipe for potential high returns. If you missed the chance to buy Bitcoin when it was $100, you can still comfort yourself with the knowledge that plenty of people also ignored Amazon when it was selling books out of Jeff Bezos's garage.

Adoption: From Skepticism to Seriousness

Remember when people thought email was a fad, and now it's how you find out your electricity bill is overdue? Cryptocurrency is following a similar path. What started as an obscure internet experiment is now being embraced by major companies, financial institutions, and even governments. El Salvador made headlines by adopting Bitcoin as legal tender (yes, you can buy tacos with it there), and big-name companies like Tesla and PayPal are integrating cryptocurrency into their ecosystems.

This growing adoption signals a shift from "weird internet money" to "mainstream financial tool." Every time a Fortune 500 company adds crypto to its balance sheet, it adds a layer of legitimacy to the entire ecosystem—and, frankly, a little FOMO (fear of missing out) for the rest of us.

An Alternative to Traditional 'Value' Assets

Let's face it—investing in traditional value assets like gold and real estate can feel like dating in your 30s: everyone's already taken, and the prices are ridiculously high. Cryptocurrency offers a fresh alternative for those looking to diversify their portfolios. While gold shines (literally), it doesn't have the technological innovation or potential for exponential growth that crypto offers. And while real estate is great, you can't exactly store a few Bitcoin in your back pocket without paying property taxes.

Crypto potentially provides a hedge against inflation (take that, fiat currency!) and opens the door to global accessibility. It's the democratization of wealth, allowing anyone with a smartphone to participate in markets that were once reserved for the elite. Plus, you don't need a metal detector or a down payment—just an internet connection and the guts to ride the waves of market volatility.

Revolutionizing Business Through Blockchain

Cryptocurrency isn't just about creating digital wealth—it's part of a larger technological revolution powered by blockchain. Imagine a world where contracts execute themselves, supply chains are fully transparent, and international payments happen in seconds instead of weeks. That's the kind of change blockchain technology is driving. And owning cryptocurrency is like buying a ticket to this transformative show.

Ethereum, for example, isn't just a currency; it's a platform enabling decentralized apps, smart contracts, and entire ecosystems. Other blockchains are tackling issues like secure identity verification, data privacy, and even voting systems. It's like watching the internet being built all over again—except this time, you can invest directly in the infrastructure.

The Challenge of High-Stakes Innovation

Of course, investing in cryptocurrency isn't without its quirks. One moment, you're checking your portfolio and feeling like a financial genius; the next, you're Googling, "Why is my cryptocurrency crashing?" It's not for the faint of heart, but the potential for high returns is undeniable. And let's be real—how many times in history do you get the chance to invest in something that's both revolutionary and still slightly baffling to your grandparents?

Whether you're drawn to the scarcity, the adoption, the diversification, or the tech revolution, cryptocurrency offers a unique opportunity. It's like betting on the future of money, commerce, and innovation—all rolled into one digital asset. Just remember to hold on tight, because the ride will definitely have a few loops and twists. But hey, isn't that what makes it fun?

The Risks of Cryptocurrency: High Stakes in the Wild West

Investing in cryptocurrency can feel like discovering a new frontier—exciting, full of opportunity, and just a little dangerous. For every story of someone turning $100 into millions, there's a cautionary tale of someone else losing their life savings because they forgot their wallet password or fell for a scam. Cryptocurrencies come with undeniable potential, but they also carry risks that could send even the most seasoned investor into a spiral of regret Googling, *"Why did my portfolio just implode?"* Let's explore these risks, from the whiplash-inducing volatility to the looming shadow of government regulation, and everything in between.

Volatility: The Rollercoaster You Didn't Ask For

If you're prone to motion sickness, the cryptocurrency market might not be for you. Prices can swing wildly in a matter of hours—Bitcoin alone has seen single-day price drops of 20% or more, the kind of drama that would make even the stock market clutch its pearls. One moment, you're bragging to your friends about your "moonshot," and the next, you're refreshing your portfolio with the grim determination of someone watching a train wreck in slow motion.

Volatility is driven by everything from tweets (thanks, Elon) to speculative trading and a general lack of stabilizing forces like dividends or earnings reports. It's exhilarating on the way up, but don't forget to buckle in for the inevitable dips.

Security: Hackers, Scammers, and Wallet Woes

Cryptocurrencies are often touted as secure, but only if you're careful. The technology behind them—blockchain—is indeed robust, but human error remains the Achilles' heel. Forget your wallet password? Too bad, those coins are gone forever. Fall for a phishing scam? Say goodbye to your holdings. Hackers have stolen billions from exchanges, wallets, and unsuspecting investors.

Even so-called "safe" practices like using hardware wallets can go awry if you lose the device or forget where you stashed the recovery key. It's like the world's most high-stakes treasure hunt, except the treasure is your money, and the map is written in disappearing ink.

Lack of Intrinsic Value: A Digital Mirage?

Critics love to point out that cryptocurrencies, unlike stocks or bonds, have no intrinsic value. They don't represent ownership in a company or pay dividends. Bitcoin isn't backed by a government, a shiny bar of gold, or even a promise from a friendly stranger. Its value comes entirely from what people are willing to pay for it. Some call it the ultimate free market; others call it a bubble waiting to pop. Either way, you're betting that the collective belief in cryptocurrency doesn't waver—because if it does, the whole house of digital cards could collapse.

Usability and Liquidity: Still a Work in Progress

Despite its buzz, cryptocurrency is still far from replacing your debit card. Sure, you can use Bitcoin to buy a Tesla (if Elon Musk is in the mood), but for most day-to-day transactions, it's easier to stick with cash or credit. The infrastructure for widespread usability just isn't there yet, and even where it is, the transaction fees can make you wince. Sending $20 in Ethereum? That'll be $50 in gas fees, thank you very much.

Liquidity can also be an issue. Smaller or less popular cryptocurrencies might be hard to sell without taking a steep discount. The result? You could end up holding onto coins you'd rather ditch, like a digital bag of Beanie Babies nobody wants anymore.

Developing Support Structure: A Market Still Taking Shape

The infrastructure supporting cryptocurrency is still evolving, and growing pains are inevitable. Exchanges crash during high-volume trading, wallets get hacked, and new projects sometimes vanish overnight. Even major players like FTX, under Sam Bankman-Fried, have suffered catastrophic failures. FTX's collapse highlighted a troubling lack of risk management and accountability, leaving investors empty-handed and shaking confidence in the market.

A key issue is the lack of regulatory oversight. Unlike traditional financial markets monitored by the SEC or CFTC, crypto operates with minimal supervision, allowing platforms to cut corners or engage in questionable practices. While the promise of decentralization drives innovation, it also leaves investors vulnerable to mismanagement and fraud. Until the market matures and clearer safeguards are in place, crypto investors must tread carefully, knowing the support structure is still a work in progress.

Regulatory Impacts: The Elephant in the Blockchain

Perhaps the biggest risk looming over cryptocurrency is government regulation—or outright bans. Sovereign nations have a vested interest in protecting their monetary monopolies, and cryptocurrency poses a direct challenge. Take China, for example, which banned Bitcoin mining and transactions, sending shockwaves through the market. Other countries, while less aggressive, are imposing stricter regulations on trading, reporting, and taxation.

It's not hard to see why. Governments can't easily track or control cryptocurrency transactions, which makes them nervous. After all, who needs pesky things like centralized authority when you can have decentralized chaos? The question isn't *if* more regulations will come but *when* and *how severe* they'll be. And let's not forget the possibility of Central Bank Digital Currencies (CBDCs)—government-issued cryptocurrencies—which could further dampen enthusiasm for decentralized options.

For investors, this means navigating a regulatory minefield. Will the U.S. crack down on crypto exchanges? Could Europe impose sweeping restrictions? The answers are as uncertain as Bitcoin's price on any given Tuesday.

How to Get Started with Cryptocurrency

Assuming you are comfortable with the risks and still want to join the party, investing in cryptocurrency is more accessible than ever. Here's how to begin:

1. **Choose a Platform**: Popular exchanges like **Coinbase**, **Binance**, and **Kraken** offer user-friendly interfaces for buying and trading cryptocurrencies. For those who prefer a mobile-first approach, apps like **Robinhood** or **Cash App** allow you to dip your toes into the market.

2. **Select a Wallet**: A cryptocurrency wallet is where you store your digital assets. Wallets can be online (hot wallets) or offline (cold wallets). While hot wallets are convenient, cold wallets like **Ledger** or **Trezor** are more secure for long-term storage.

3. **Start Small**: Given crypto's volatility, it's wise to begin with a modest investment—an amount you're willing to lose. Platforms like Coinbase allow you to buy fractions of a Bitcoin or Ethereum, making crypto accessible to all budgets.

4. **Research Your Assets**: Not all cryptocurrencies are created equal. Before investing, understand the project's use case, team, and roadmap. Bitcoin and Ethereum are generally considered safer bets due to their established track records and widespread adoption.

Ethereum: The Swiss Army Knife of Crypto

While Bitcoin gets all the headlines as the "king of crypto," Ethereum is the tech-savvy sibling quietly building an empire. Unlike Bitcoin, which primarily functions as digital gold, Ethereum is more like a bustling city where developers can create decentralized applications (dApps), smart contracts, and even entire ecosystems. Think of it as a platform where blockchain technology really flexes its muscles. Want to create your own cryptocurrency? Host a decentralized crowdfunding campaign? Run a virtual art gallery? Ethereum's got you covered.

At the heart of Ethereum is its programmable blockchain, which allows for self-executing smart contracts. These are like vending machines of the financial world: they perform specific actions when predefined conditions are met, with no middleman required. Need tickets to a concert? A smart contract could handle the sale, verify the buyer, and even send your refund if the show gets canceled. Ethereum also recently moved to a proof-of-stake model, meaning it's more eco-friendly than Bitcoin's energy-guzzling proof-of-work system. If Bitcoin is the traditionalist, Ethereum is the innovative millennial asking, "But what if we could do more?"

Other Coins: The Rest of the Crypto Zoo

Beyond Bitcoin and Ethereum, the cryptocurrency market is home to thousands of coins, each vying for attention like contestants on a blockchain-themed reality show. Some have legitimate use cases, while others are little more than digital memes with marketing budgets. Let's explore a few of the larger players that are worth knowing.

Binance Coin (BNB) is the utility token of Binance, one of the world's largest crypto exchanges. Initially created to reduce transaction fees on the platform, BNB has grown into a multi-purpose token used for payments, investments, and even booking vacations. It's like Bitcoin's practical cousin who always has a coupon for dinner.

Cardano (ADA), often described as a more academic approach to blockchain, focuses on sustainability and scalability. Its development is backed by peer-reviewed research, which sounds fancy but basically means they take their time to get things right. It's the blockchain equivalent of someone who doesn't rush to put out a sloppy product just to hit a deadline.

Solana (SOL) is all about speed. Known for processing thousands of transactions per second with low fees, it's often compared to Ethereum but faster and cheaper. Of course, it's also had its share of hiccups, including network outages. Think of Solana as a high-performance sports car: impressive when it works, but occasionally stuck in the shop.

Ripple (XRP) is designed for cross-border payments, aiming to replace slow, expensive systems like SWIFT. It's popular with banks and financial institutions, which gives it a different vibe from the decentralized ethos of other cryptocurrencies. If Bitcoin is the rebel and Ethereum is the innovator, Ripple is the corporate go-getter in a tailored suit.

The beauty (and chaos) of these coins lies in their diversity. Each has its own strengths, weaknesses, and quirks, catering to specific audiences or industries. Whether you're looking for innovation, speed, or utility, there's a coin for everyone. Just remember, for every Cardano or Solana, there's a "Shiba Inu"—a coin that started as a joke but somehow made a few people millionaires. Welcome to the unpredictable world of altcoins, where every coin has a story, and not all of them end happily.

Case Study: The Pizza That Could've Bought a Mansion

In the annals of cryptocurrency history, one story stands out as both a cautionary tale and a hilarious reminder of the early days of Bitcoin: the infamous Bitcoin pizza purchase. On May 22, 2010, Laszlo Hanyecz, a programmer and early Bitcoin enthusiast, made what is widely considered the first real-world cryptocurrency transaction. He traded 10,000 Bitcoin for two large pizzas from Papa John's. At the time, those coins were worth about $40—an exchange that seemed fair for a couple of cheesy, carb-loaded meals.

Fast forward to today, and those 10,000 Bitcoin would be worth hundreds of millions of dollars. That's right—those pizzas now hold the dubious honor of being the most expensive meal ever consumed, at least in retrospect. Hanyecz, to his credit, doesn't seem to regret the decision, often saying he's just glad to have been part of Bitcoin's history. After all, someone had to prove Bitcoin could be used for something other than hypothetical internet discussions.

The Bitcoin pizza story illustrates two critical points about cryptocurrency. First, its early adopters were visionaries who took risks long before Bitcoin had any real value. Second, it highlights the volatility and unpredictability of crypto as an investment. One day, it's pizza money; the next, it's generational wealth.

It also underscores the importance of thinking long-term in the crypto space. While it's tempting to cash out when your holdings can buy you a flashy new toy, the potential upside of holding onto the right coins at the right time can be astronomical. Of course, hindsight is 20/20, and nobody can perfectly time the market. But the Bitcoin pizza story is a testament to the transformative power of cryptocurrency—and a reminder to always think twice before trading your digital gold for a pepperoni slice.

Rates of Return: Bitcoin and Ethereum's Journey to the Moon

When it comes to eye-popping returns, Bitcoin and Ethereum are the undisputed poster children of cryptocurrency. These digital assets have delivered returns so extraordinary that they've turned everyday investors into millionaires—and, in some cases, billionaires. But before you imagine yourself retiring on a tropical island, it's worth diving into the history of these returns, the forces driving them, and the volatility that makes crypto a wild ride.

Bitcoin: The Original Moonshot

Bitcoin, launched in 2009, started at a value so low that early transactions were measured in fractions of a penny. For years, it was the plaything of tech geeks and internet libertarians, seen as an experiment rather than an investment. Then, in 2010, the infamous pizza purchase pegged Bitcoin's value at roughly $0.004 per coin. Fast forward to December 2024, and Bitcoin has reached new all-time highs, with prices exceeding $100,000.

This meteoric rise represents an astronomical return on investment. To put that in perspective, a $100 investment in Bitcoin in 2010 would now be worth over $2.5 billion. Let that sink in.

But Bitcoin's journey hasn't been without turbulence. The coin's price has experienced dramatic swings, with drops as severe as 80% during bear markets. As of today, Bitcoin continues to hover as the flagship of cryptocurrency, but its meteoric rise is a double-edged sword: it's both a symbol of crypto's potential and a cautionary tale about extreme volatility.

Ethereum: The Multi-Purpose Powerhouse

Ethereum entered the scene in 2015 with a vision to go beyond Bitcoin's digital gold narrative. Launched at an initial price of around $0.30 during its presale, Ethereum quickly gained traction as a platform for decentralized applications and smart contracts. By December 2024, Ethereum has reached new heights, with prices around $4,000.

Ethereum's growth has been driven by its utility. As the backbone for NFTs, DeFi platforms, and countless blockchain projects, Ethereum has become an indispensable part of the crypto ecosystem. Unlike Bitcoin, which relies on its narrative of scarcity, Ethereum's value is tied to its usability. Developers and projects need Ether (ETH) to pay for transactions on the network, creating a constant stream of demand. Its recent shift to a proof-of-stake model has also made it more energy-efficient, potentially attracting environmentally conscious investors.

The Big Picture: Returns and Risks

Both Bitcoin and Ethereum have delivered returns that make traditional investments like stocks or real estate look downright boring. But with those high returns come high risks. The volatility that makes crypto so exciting is the same factor that causes sleepless nights for investors. Prices can rise or fall dramatically in response to everything from regulatory news to a billionaire's tweet.

For those who got in early, Bitcoin and Ethereum represent life-changing opportunities. For everyone else, they're a lesson in the power of timing—and the patience required to hold on through the market's inevitable ups and downs. While past performance is no guarantee of future results, the incredible rates of return on Bitcoin and Ethereum have solidified their status as two of the most transformative investments of the 21st century. Just remember: with great returns comes great responsibility—and maybe a little antacid for the stomach-churning volatility.

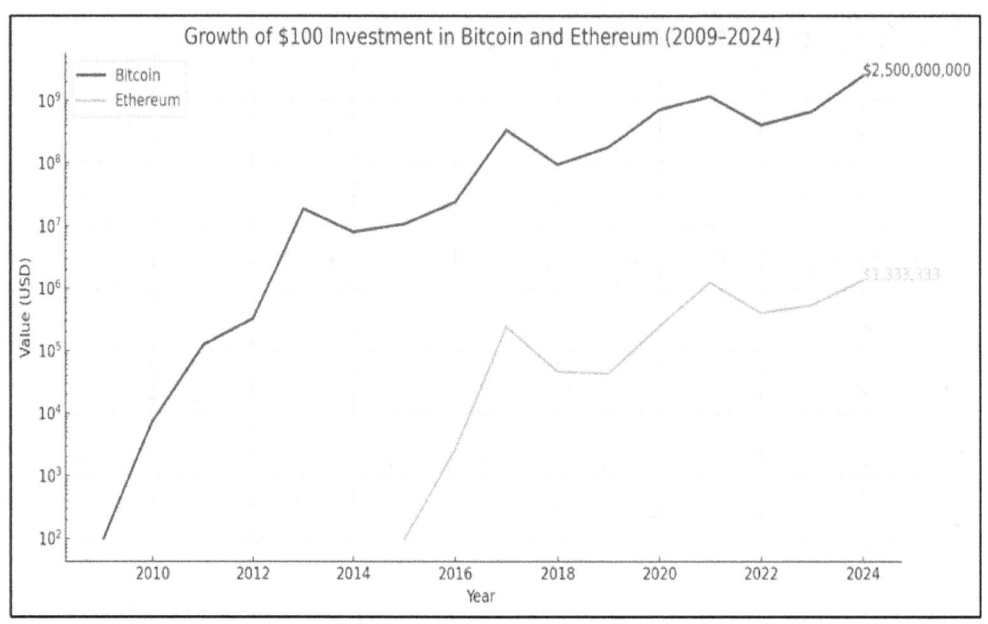

Figure 13: $100 Invested in Bitcoin and Ethereum Since Inception

Risk Assessment: Crypto's Place in Your Portfolio

On our **Risk Scale**, cryptocurrencies rank between **4 and 5** due to their extreme volatility and speculative nature. Established assets like Bitcoin and Ethereum fall on the lower end of the spectrum, while altcoins and NFTs occupy the higher end. Crypto can be a valuable diversification tool, but it should represent a small portion of your overall portfolio.

Final Thoughts

Cryptocurrency is one of the most exciting—and polarizing—investment opportunities of our time. For believers, it represents the future of money and the dawn of a decentralized financial system. For skeptics, it's a bubble waiting to burst. The truth likely lies somewhere in between.

Whether you're investing in Bitcoin as "digital gold" or exploring the wild world of altcoins and NFTs, cryptocurrency demands careful research, disciplined risk management, and a willingness to weather volatility. For those who embrace its potential, crypto can be a thrilling—and potentially lucrative—addition to a diversified portfolio. Just remember: invest only what you're prepared to lose, and enjoy the ride.

The Wide World of Other Investments

Investing isn't limited to the familiar worlds of stocks, bonds, and real estate—it's a vast landscape filled with creative and unconventional opportunities. For beginners and seasoned investors alike, venturing into lesser-known options can unlock potential for growth, enjoyment, and diversification. From lending money directly to small businesses to staking claims in emerging industries or even exploring sustainable ventures like green energy funds, there are countless ways to make your money work for you. In this chapter, we'll introduce you to the wide world of alternative investments not covered elsewhere in this book, helping you discover new ways to build wealth while keeping your investment journey exciting and adaptable to your interests.

Buying a Business: A Turnkey Investment (Sometimes)

Purchasing an existing business is one of the most straightforward ways to dive into entrepreneurship. Whether it's a local coffee shop with a loyal customer base or a small manufacturing firm cranking out widgets, you're buying something with an established track record—hopefully. The pros are clear: you're stepping into a venture that already has customers, revenue, and a functioning operation. It's like buying a car that's already been broken in but still runs smoothly.

But there are cons, too. What if the coffee shop's charm relies entirely on the outgoing owner's barista skills and quirky jokes? What if that manufacturing firm comes with a mountain of debt you didn't see buried in the fine print? Buying a business requires thorough due diligence, which is a fancy way of saying, "Get a lawyer and an accountant, stat." If you find the right business, it can be a goldmine. If you don't, it might turn into a full-time stress machine.

Franchise Purchases: Freedom with a Side of Rules

If buying a business feels like too much of a gamble, a franchise might seem like the safer bet. After all, you're investing in a proven system, whether it's flipping burgers or running a fitness studio. You get the brand recognition, the playbook, and sometimes even the training. It's like painting by numbers—everything's laid out for you.

But don't get too excited just yet. Franchises come with strings attached, and by "strings," I mean rules. Lots and lots of rules. From how much you can charge for a burger to where you buy your ketchup, franchises dictate almost every aspect of the operation. That recognizable logo? You'll pay for it—often through hefty franchise fees and ongoing royalties. Supplies? You'll likely be required to buy them from the franchise-approved vendor, which may not be the cheapest option. The lack of control can be frustrating for someone with entrepreneurial flair, but if you're okay following orders in exchange for a more predictable investment, franchises can be a solid choice.

Private Lending: Be the Bank (Kind Of)

If owning a business isn't your thing, how about financing someone else's dreams? Private lending lets you play the role of the bank, earning interest by loaning money directly to individuals or small businesses. You can go the one-on-one route, loaning to a friend (proceed with caution) or a vetted borrower. Alternatively, you can lend through crowdfunding platforms like LendingClub or Prosper, which pool your money with other investors to fund loans.

The pros? It's a way to earn passive income without the headaches of running a business. The cons? Borrowers don't always repay their loans, and you could end up with less money than you started with. Diversification is key here—don't put all your eggs in the "Bob's Cat Café" basket. But when done carefully, private lending can offer steady returns and the satisfaction of helping someone else succeed. Just remember, you're not Santa Claus, so vet your borrowers like your money depends on it—because it does.

The Final Thought: A World of Options

These investments barely scratch the surface of what's out there. From flipping domain names to angel investing in startups, the possibilities are endless. Each comes with its own risks, rewards, and quirks, but that's the beauty of investing: there's no one-size-fits-all solution. Whether you're buying a coffee shop, signing up for a franchise, or funding someone else's dream, the key is to do your homework and stay diversified. And above all, keep a sense of humor handy—because, as with all investments, things don't always go as planned. But hey, sometimes the unexpected turns out to be the best investment of all.

Commodity Futures Trading: Betting on Beans and Beyond

If you've ever wanted to invest in something a little more tangible (but still intangible in practice), commodity futures trading might be for you. While gold and silver get all the glamour, the real action happens in markets for agricultural products, energy, and industrial metals. Think soybeans, crude oil, and even frozen orange juice—yes, that's a real market, and no, it's not just a plot device from *Trading Places*. Futures trading involves contracts to buy or sell these commodities at a set price in the future, which sounds simple enough until you realize it's a high-stakes guessing game influenced by everything from weather patterns to geopolitical drama. Nail it, and you might profit handsomely; get it wrong, and you could end up with a warehouse full of corn you didn't plan on owning. It's not for the faint of heart, but for those who enjoy volatility and the thrill of a fast-paced market, commodities futures can offer unique opportunities—and a crash course in agricultural economics.

Your Journey Starts Now

Congratulations! You've made it to the end of this book, and if you're still reading, you're already ahead of the game. Most people talk about investing, maybe even dabble in a little research, but never take the plunge. You, however, have armed yourself with the knowledge to make smarter decisions about your money and your future. Now comes the hard part—and the exciting part—putting that knowledge into action.

Let's recap what we've learned. Investing isn't just for Wall Street tycoons or Silicon Valley wizards. It's for everyone. Whether you're starting with $100, $1,000, or more, there's a place for you in this game. From the stock market to real estate, collectibles, and even cryptocurrency, the world is full of opportunities to grow your wealth. The key is finding the path that aligns with your goals, your risk tolerance, and, let's be honest, your patience.

What This Book Has Taught You

Throughout these chapters, we've explored a variety of investment types, demystified complex concepts, and laid out practical strategies for beginners. We've learned that government bonds are a safe, steady option, while stocks can help you ride the waves of long-term growth. We've looked at how you can invest in yourself, perhaps the greatest investment of all, and dipped into the digital realm of cryptocurrencies and NFTs. We even ventured into the tangible world of real estate and collectibles, where your investments might come with a set of keys or a rare Charizard card.

But what's the common thread? Every investment starts with a small step. Whether it's clicking "buy" on a fractional share of your favorite stock, opening a high-yield savings account, or creating a budget to save for that first down payment, the journey begins with action.

Why Today is the Best Day to Start

Here's the thing: there's no perfect time to start investing. The markets will always be unpredictable. You'll always wish you had more money, more knowledge, more certainty. But here's a secret most seasoned investors will tell you: the best time to start was yesterday. The second-best time is today.

Investing is like planting a tree. The earlier you plant it, the more time it has to grow. Sure, there will be storms along the way—economic downturns, market corrections, maybe even a recession or two. But trees don't grow overnight, and neither does wealth. The sooner you get started, the sooner you'll reap the rewards of compounding returns, dividends, rental income, or even the occasional lucky break.

Overcoming the Excuses

If you're hesitating, you're not alone. Maybe you're worried you'll make a mistake. (Spoiler: you will. We all do.) Or maybe you feel like you don't have enough money to start. Let's bust that myth right now: you don't need thousands of dollars to invest. You can start with $100 or less. Fractional shares, robo-advisors, crowdfunding platforms—they've all made investing more accessible than ever before.

And let's not forget the other excuse: "I don't have the time." Investing doesn't have to take hours of research or constant monitoring. Start small, automate your contributions if possible, and let the magic of compounding do the heavy lifting. Your future self will thank you.

It's About More Than Money

Investing isn't just about growing your bank account—it's about taking control of your future. It's about creating options for yourself, whether that means retiring early, starting your own business, or simply enjoying a little extra financial security. It's about building something that lasts, something that works for you even while you sleep.

Think of your investments as little workers, out there in the world, earning money on your behalf. With every dollar you invest, you're sending another worker out to join the team. Over time, they'll build something remarkable.

Motivation to Start Now

Still on the fence? Let me leave you with this: you'll never regret investing in your future. Sure, there will be ups and downs. Some investments won't pan out, and that's okay. The important thing is to start. Even if it feels like a small step—a single share of an ETF, a $50 deposit into a savings account—it's a step in the right direction.

Imagine looking back in five, ten, or twenty years. Will you be glad you waited, or will you be thrilled you started? Every great investor, entrepreneur, and success story started somewhere, often with humble beginnings. The only way to grow your wealth is to begin.

So, take a deep breath. Use the Investment Checklist in the back of the book. Open that brokerage account. Research that first property. Dust off that old Pokémon card collection. Whatever your path, start walking it today.

The Power of $100

If there's one thing this book has shown, it's that $100 can go a long way—or, depending on your choices, not very far at all. Whether you're investing in Bitcoin, Beanie Babies, or a budding barista empire, $100 can be the seed of something extraordinary. Or it can disappear faster than a pizza in 2010 paid for in Bitcoin. To recap, here are just a few of the things you could do with $100:

- Buy a fraction of a Bitcoin and daydream about retiring early (while obsessively refreshing your portfolio).
- Start collecting coins, trading cards, or even NFTs, proving that scarcity and sentimentality never go out of style.
- Get your feet wet in the stock market, snagging a slice of Apple or Tesla (or at least a crumb of one, thanks to fractional shares).
- Invest in yourself with an online course, a shiny new business book, or a decent pair of running shoes.
- Fund someone else's dream (or questionable business plan) through peer-to-peer lending or crowdfunding.

The point isn't just that $100 can be stretched—it's that it can grow. Whether you're chasing massive returns, building a collection you love, or starting a journey of financial independence, small beginnings often lead to big outcomes. So, go ahead: take that $100, pick an idea from this book, and see where it takes you. Just maybe don't use it all on pizza… unless you're really hungry.

Use Our Resources

For help and access to many of the resources referenced in this book, please check out the financial website, www.nextgensage.com. This website is dedicated to helping people, like you, on their personal finance journey. The articles and resources listed here include business ideas, tools, and resources to get started.

Final Words

The world of investing can seem intimidating, but it's also full of potential. You don't have to be an expert to succeed. You just have to start. Make mistakes, learn from them, and keep going. The journey will be worth it.

Your financial future is in your hands. Whether you're investing for a dream retirement, a new business, or just a little peace of mind, the first step is always the hardest. So, go ahead—take it. The next chapter of your life is waiting to be written, and it starts with a single decision.

As they say, the best investment you can make is in yourself. And now, you're ready to do just that

Glossary of Financial Terms and Acronyms

A

- **Appreciation**: An increase in the value of an asset over time. For example, a stock may appreciate in value as the company grows.
- **Asset**: Anything of value owned by an individual or organization, including stocks, bonds, real estate, and cash.

B

- **Bond**: A fixed-income investment representing a loan made by an investor to a borrower (typically corporate or government). Bonds pay periodic interest and return the principal at maturity.
- **Brokerage Account**: An account with a licensed brokerage that allows individuals to buy and sell securities such as stocks, bonds, ETFs, and mutual funds.

C

- **Capital**: Wealth in the form of money or assets, used or accumulated for investment purposes.
- **Compounding**: The process of earning interest on both the principal amount and the accumulated interest from previous periods.
- **Certificate of Deposit (CD)**: A savings product with a fixed term and interest rate, offering higher returns than traditional savings accounts.
- **Cryptocurrency**: A digital or virtual currency that uses cryptography for security, operating on a decentralized blockchain network (e.g., Bitcoin, Ethereum).
- **Crowdfunding**: A method of raising small amounts of capital from a large number of people to fund a project or investment.

D

- **Dividend**: A portion of a company's earnings distributed to shareholders, usually as cash or additional stock.
- **Dividend Reinvestment Plan (DRIP)**: A program that allows investors to reinvest their dividends into

additional shares of the issuing company, often at no additional cost.

E

- **Equity**: Ownership interest in a company, typically represented by shares of stock.
- **Exchange-Traded Fund (ETF)**: A type of investment fund that trades on stock exchanges, combining features of stocks and mutual funds. ETFs are usually diversified and low-cost.

F

- **Federal Reserve (Fed)**: The central banking system of the United States, responsible for monetary policy and financial stability.
- **Fractional Shares**: Partial shares of a company, allowing investors to invest smaller amounts rather than buying a full share.

G

- **Government Bonds**: Debt securities issued by a government to support government spending. Examples include Treasury bonds, Treasury notes, and Treasury bills.

- **Gig Economy**: A labor market characterized by short-term or freelance work, often facilitated by online platforms.

I

- **Inflation**: The rate at which the general level of prices for goods and services rises, eroding purchasing power over time.
- **Investment-Grade Bonds**: High-quality bonds rated BBB or higher by credit rating agencies, indicating low risk of default.

L

- **Leverage**: The use of borrowed capital to increase potential returns on investment. Real estate investors often use leverage through mortgages.
- **Liquidity**: The ease with which an asset can be converted into cash without significantly affecting its price.

M

- **Market Volatility**: The rate at which the price of securities increases or decreases over a certain period of time. High volatility means prices can change dramatically.

- **Mutual Fund**: An investment vehicle pooling funds from multiple investors to purchase securities, professionally managed and diversified.

N

- **Non-Fungible Token (NFT)**: A unique digital asset representing ownership of a specific item or piece of content, verified using blockchain technology.

P

- **Portfolio**: A collection of financial investments such as stocks, bonds, real estate, and other assets.
- **Principal**: The initial amount of money invested or loaned, excluding interest or earnings.

R

- **Real Estate Investment Trust (REIT)**: A company that owns, operates, or finances income-generating real estate. REITs allow investors to buy shares in a diversified real estate portfolio.

- **Risk Tolerance**: An individual's willingness and ability to endure market volatility and investment losses.
- **Risk Scale (0-5)**: A rating system used in this book to measure the risk to capital in various investment types, with 0 representing no risk and 5 representing very high risk.

S

- **Savings Bond**: A government-issued bond designed for individual investors, often offering fixed interest and inflation protection.
- **Stock**: A type of security representing ownership in a company, entitling the holder to a portion of its earnings and assets.
- **Stock Option**: A financial derivative that gives an investor the right, but not the obligation, to buy or sell a stock at a set price within a specified period.

T

- **Technical Analysis**: A method of evaluating securities by analyzing statistical trends from trading activity, such as price movements and volume.

- **TreasuryDirect**: An online platform provided by the U.S. government for purchasing Treasury securities directly.

Y

- **Yield**: The income generated by an investment, usually expressed as a percentage of the investment's current value or cost.

Investment Checklist

This investment checklist serves as a practical guide to help you evaluate and choose investments based on the principles covered in this book. Use it as a reference before committing to any new opportunity.

1. Define Your Investment Goals

Before choosing an investment, clarify what you want to achieve:

- ☐ **Short-Term Goals**: Build an emergency fund, save for a trip, or fund a purchase within 1-3 years.
- ☐ **Medium-Term Goals**: Save for a down payment, start a business, or plan for major expenses (3-10 years).
- ☐ **Long-Term Goals**: Retirement, financial independence, or funding children's education (10+ years).

Goal: _____

Time Horizon: _____

2. Assess Your Risk Tolerance

Determine your comfort level with potential losses and market volatility:

- ☐ **Low Risk (1-2)**: Investments with stable returns and minimal risk to capital.
- ☐ **Moderate Risk (3)**: Balanced risk with reasonable growth opportunities.
- ☐ **High Risk (4-5)**: Higher returns possible but with significant volatility and potential loss.

Risk Tolerance Level: _____

3. Choose Your Investment Type

Identify which investment category aligns with your goals, capital, and risk tolerance:

- ☐ **Government Securities**: Treasury bonds, savings bonds (low risk).
- ☐ **Savings Accounts/CDs**: For safety, liquidity, and guaranteed returns.
- ☐ **Gold and Silver**: A hedge against inflation and economic uncertainty.

- ☐ **Corporate Bonds**: Fixed-income returns with moderate risk.
- ☐ **Stock Market**: Long-term growth through stocks, ETFs, and index funds.
- ☐ **Real Estate**: Rental properties, crowdfunding platforms, or REITs.
- ☐ **Collectibles**: Coins, trading cards, art, or sneakers.
- ☐ **Cryptocurrency**: High-risk investments like Bitcoin or Ethereum.
- ☐ **Yourself**: Side hustles, education, or entrepreneurship.

Chosen Investment Type: _____

4. Evaluate Capital Requirements

Ask yourself:

- ☐ What is the minimum investment required?
- ☐ Can I start small (e.g., fractional shares, ETFs, or crowdfunding)?
- ☐ Do I have enough funds to cover transaction fees, taxes, or additional costs?

- ☐ If required, how long will it take to save up the initial capital?

Investment Minimum: _____

Available Capital: _____

5. Research the Investment

Gather key details to make an informed decision:

- ☐ **Historical Performance**: How has this investment performed over 5-10 years?
- ☐ **Returns**: Is the expected return reasonable and aligned with your goals?
- Stocks: Growth or dividends?
- Bonds: Yield and coupon rate?
- Real Estate: Rental income vs. appreciation?
- ☐ **Liquidity**: Can I sell or cash out easily if needed?
- ☐ **Fees**: What are the associated fees (management fees, trading fees, taxes)?
- ☐ **Risk Factors**: What risks are involved (market risk, inflation risk, default risk, etc.)?

Summary of Research:

_____

_____

6. Evaluate the Risk vs. Reward

Based on your research, determine:

- ☐ The **potential upside**: What's the maximum realistic return?
- ☐ The **downside risk**: What's the likelihood of losing capital?
- ☐ The **risk/reward ratio**: Does the return justify the risk?

Risk/Reward Assessment: _____

7. Understand Your Timeline

Match your investment horizon to the type of investment:

- ☐ Short-Term (<3 years): Savings accounts, CDs, Treasury securities.
- ☐ Medium-Term (3-10 years): ETFs, REITs, bonds, or balanced funds.
- ☐ Long-Term (10+ years): Stocks, real estate, collectibles, or gold.

Time Horizon: _____

8. Diversify Your Portfolio

Ensure your investments are spread across asset classes to reduce risk:

- ☐ Stocks or ETFs for growth.
- ☐ Bonds or government securities for safety and fixed income.
- ☐ Real estate or REITs for stability and income.
- ☐ Alternative assets like gold, collectibles, or cryptocurrency for diversification.

How Diversified Am I?

☐ Very Diversified | ☐ Somewhat Diversified | ☐ Not Diversified

9. Start Small and Monitor Regularly

- ☐ Start with a small investment to test the waters.
- ☐ Use tools like robo-advisors, brokerage dashboards, or spreadsheets to track progress.
- ☐ Monitor performance quarterly or annually and adjust if needed.

Next Steps: _____

10. Take Action

The hardest part of investing is taking the first step. Review your checklist and ask yourself:

- **Is this investment aligned with my goals?**
- **Do I understand the risks and rewards?**
- **Am I ready to start today?**

If the answer is "yes," then **take action now**. Open that account, buy that first share, or fund that real estate project. The earlier you start, the sooner you'll see results.

Final Reminder

✓ **Stay Consistent**: Small, regular investments add up over time.

✓ **Stay Educated**: Markets evolve—keep learning.

✓ **Stay Patient**: Wealth takes time to grow.

Your journey starts with one step. Let today be the day you take it.

Example Investment Plan Summary

Investor Name:

Jane Smith

Investment Goal:

Build a diversified investment portfolio to achieve financial independence in 20 years with a focus on steady growth and manageable risk.

1. Investment Goals

- **Primary Goal:** Save and grow investments to achieve $1,000,000 in assets over 20 years.
- **Secondary Goal:** Generate passive income of at least $2,500/month in retirement through dividends, real estate income, and other investment streams.
- **Short-Term Goal (1-3 Years):** Build an emergency fund of $10,000.
- **Medium-Term Goal (3-10 Years):** Save $50,000 for a down payment on an investment property.

2. Investment Time Horizon

- **Short-Term Needs:** Emergency fund (cash/safe investments).
- **Medium-Term Needs:** Down payment and income-focused investments.
- **Long-Term Plan (20 Years):** Focus on growth investments to benefit from compounding.

3. Risk Tolerance

- **Risk Level:** Moderate (Risk Scale: 3/5)
- Jane is comfortable with moderate market fluctuations in exchange for long-term growth, provided her core investments are diversified and balanced.

4. Current Financial Position

- **Starting Capital:** $5,000
- **Monthly Contributions:** $500
- **Existing Debt:** None
- **Emergency Fund:** $2,500 saved so far

5. Investment Allocation

Investment Type

Target Allocation

Details

Stocks/ETFs - 50%

- Focus on broad market ETFs like S&P 500 (e.g., VOO, SPY).

- Growth stocks (Apple, Microsoft) for long-term appreciation.

- Dividend stocks (Johnson & Johnson, Coca-Cola) for passive income.

Bonds - 15%

- Government bonds for safety and fixed income.

- Investment-grade corporate bonds for moderate returns.

Real Estate - 20%

- Real Estate Investment Trusts (REITs) like VNQ for exposure to income-generating properties.

- Crowdfunding platforms (e.g., Fundrise) with low entry points.

Gold/Silver - 5%

- Physical gold and ETFs like GLD for inflation protection.

Cryptocurrency -5%

- Bitcoin (BTC) and Ethereum (ETH) for speculative high-growth opportunities.

Cash/Savings - 5%

- Maintain cash for emergency fund and short-term liquidity needs.

6. Investment Timeline and Contributions

- **Year 1-3:** Focus on building an emergency fund to $10,000. Invest in a mix of index funds (ETFs) and dividend-paying stocks with monthly contributions of $500. Add small positions in cryptocurrency.
- **Year 4-10:** Increase monthly contributions to $750 as income grows. Begin investing in real estate via crowdfunding or a down payment for a rental property. Continue holding ETFs and adding dividend stocks.

- *The Simple Path to Wealth* by JL Collins

Websites and Platforms

- **Investopedia**: Authoritative definitions and investment guides.
- **Morningstar**: Analysis of stocks, mutual funds, and ETFs.
- **TreasuryDirect**: Official platform for U.S. government securities.
- **Coinbase**: Cryptocurrency exchange and educational tools.
- **Fundrise** and **RealtyMogul**: Real estate crowdfunding platforms.
- **OpenSea** and **NonFungible.com**: NFT trading and valuation resources.
- **Heritage Auctions** and **PCGS**: Marketplaces and tools for collectible valuations.

Market Data and Economic Reports

- Federal Reserve Economic Data (FRED)
- Bloomberg
- World Bank

Sources and Methods

The material in this book has been developed through a combination of classic investment literature, modern financial resources, and emerging tools. To ensure clarity, accuracy, and accessibility, the collection of information and the writing process were assisted by advanced artificial intelligence software, including **ChatGPT 4.0**, **Grok 2.0**, **Copilot**, and **Grammarly**. These tools provided support in research synthesis, editing, and refining content to deliver an engaging and well-organized guide.

Below is a summary of the key references and resources that informed the content of this book:

Books

- *The Intelligent Investor* by Benjamin Graham
- *Common Stocks and Uncommon Profits* by Philip A. Fisher
- *The Millionaire Real Estate Investor* by Gary Keller
- *The Bitcoin Standard* by Saifedean Ammous
- *Your Money or Your Life* by Vicki Robin
- *Rich Dad Poor Dad* by Robert Kiyosaki

3. **Long-Term Focus**: Hold investments for at least 10-20 years to benefit from market growth and compounding.
4. **Diversification**: Spread investments across multiple asset classes (stocks, bonds, real estate, and gold).
5. **Emergency Fund Priority**: Build and maintain a cash buffer to avoid withdrawing from investments during market downturns.

Summary of Results (Projected)

- **Year 1**: $5,000 initial capital + $6,000 contributions = **$11,000** invested (growth approx. $12,000).
- **Year 5**: Approx. **$40,000** invested, benefiting from compounding and dividend reinvestments.
- **Year 10**: Approx. **$120,000** portfolio value, including real estate and diversified assets.
- **Year 20**: Projected portfolio value of **$1,000,000+**, assuming 8% annual returns and consistent contributions.

- **Year 10-20:** Diversify further into REITs and increase bond holdings for safety. Reinvest dividends and real estate income into growth-focused assets to maximize compounding.

7. Monitoring and Adjustments

- **Portfolio Review:** Review the portfolio **quarterly** to check performance and rebalance annually to maintain target allocations.
- **Performance Goals:** Aim for an **average annual return of 8%**, adjusting as market conditions change.
- **Adjustments:** Increase contributions when income rises, shift to more conservative assets (bonds, REITs) as retirement approaches.

8. Key Strategies

1. **Dollar-Cost Averaging**: Invest $500 monthly into diversified ETFs and stocks to reduce market timing risk.
2. **Dividend Reinvestment**: Use DRIPs to compound returns from dividend-paying stocks.

Inspirational and Educational Resources

- Warren Buffett's Annual Letters to Shareholders
- *The Simple Path to Wealth* by JL Collins
- *Rich Dad Poor Dad* by Robert Kiyosaki

This book represents a blend of timeless investment wisdom and modern insights, supported by both human expertise and the cutting-edge capabilities of artificial intelligence tools. The goal is to provide you, the reader, with a resource that is practical, informative, and relevant to your financial journey.

www.ingramcontent.com/pod-product-compliance
Lightning Source LLC
Chambersburg PA
CBHW062213220526
45471CB00009B/3186